JUNIOR MINING

INVESTOR

JUNIOR MINING

INVESTOR

14 NATURAL RESOURCE EXPERTS SHOW YOU HOW TO INVEST PROFITABLY IN EMERGING GOLD, SILVER, PLATINUM, BASE METALS, AND URANIUM MINING AND EXPLORATION STOCKS

Kevin Corcoran

For all inquiries concerning this book please send an email to:
juniormininginvestor@gmail.com

Library of Congress Cataloging-in-Publication Data:

Corcoran, Kevin, 1980-
        Junior mining investor: 14 natural resource experts show you how to invest profitably in emerging gold, silver, platinum, base metals, and uranium mining and exploration stocks / Kevin Corcoran

        1. Investing 2. Gold 3. Mining Stocks 4. Natural Resources
5. Uranium 6. Base Metals I. Title

ISBN 978-0-9795335-01

Printed in the United States of America by Bang Printing

This book is dedicated to all future Junior Mining Investors, my family, and love, Jenny.

Contents

Intro

Your Natural Resource
Investing Roadmap

The resource sector has experienced numerous booms and busts over the past centuries. Lean times lead to consolidation as the number of producers decrease and production falls. At some point, inventories tighten, and demand drives prices relatively higher once again—launching mining and exploration stocks into their next bull market cycle.

We are currently in a long-term secular bull market for nearly all commodities. With many precious metals, base metals and energy metals at all time highs; one only has to look at the phenomenal growth in China, India, Brazil, Russia, and other countries in Asia, Eastern Europe and South America. To fuel economic expansion, these countries must import massive amounts of steel, copper, aluminum, nickel, lead, zinc, natural gas, oil, and lumber. As more people are able to afford new homes, automobiles and a general higher standard of living, they also purchase more gold and silver as jewelry and for economic security. Prosperity fuels price appreciation.

This does not take into account demand from developed nations. Since the turn of the century, much of the world has experienced a bull market in housing, helping generate strong demand in base metals, lumber and other commodity sub-sectors. In the mean time, many Western countries have plans to overhaul aging energy, water and transportation infrastructure—all requiring massive amounts of metal.

Since the beginning of 2003, the Toronto Stock Exchange has been on a tear—more than doubling from 6,500 to 14,000 points. The TSX–Venture Exchange, where many junior exploration companies raise capital by going public, has also outperformed, rising from 1,500 to 3,300 during the same period. Both exchanges are heavily weighted in commodity-related companies and when they appreciate, mining and explorations stocks are moving higher.

A small number of mining majors have dominated the landscape in the past three decades. Led by mergers and acquisitions, these global mining giants have grown by buying out producing companies and those juniors with proven ore bodies. Over the last few years, investments in producing majors have proven very profitable. However, some of these companies have moved up to levels that don't leave a lot of room for further appreciation.

One area where investors can still find exceptional value is in exploration and developmental mining companies. These stocks are too small and lack the trading volume big funds need to invest in. As a result, investors and speculators can get in and out without much difficulty and before the 'general' public catches on.

Junior mining stocks can trade anywhere from a few cents to a few dollars. It is not uncommon for these stocks to double in one trading session and produce returns of 10 times your investment or more over a short period of time. It is the nature of these stocks to be very volatile and with the opportunity to make outsized returns, comes the real possibility of losing some or all of your investment. For this reason, this sector should only be approached with speculative funds—not money you can't afford to lose. Fortunately, there are strategies to help minimize risk and position yourself for windfall profits.

In *Junior Mining Investor*, 14 mining and precious metals industry analysts reveal their specific tips, strategies, ideas, and processes to evaluate and make money in mining and exploration stocks. These authors are newsletter writers with thousands of loyal readers, fund managers in charge of multi-million dollar accounts and investors who have succeeded in past bull markets and survived through the inevitable downturns that follow. Bottom line, they've helped many investors create great wealth and want to show you how to do the same.

Here are some of the things these professionals teach you in this book:

- The functions of various metals in financial markets and economies and how to gauge their demand to create trading opportunities
- How to interpret drill results and assays to know when a stock has the best chance to rapidly appreciate
- Why the uranium bull market is underway and how to identify companies that will profit from the boom
- What technical formations to look for in mining and exploration stocks
- How to manage portfolio risk in speculative mining shares
- The different types of mineral deposits and what grades of gold, silver, platinum, base metals, and uranium that are currently being mined
- How to invest in Canadian and Australian equities
- What you need from an exploration company's management team before you invest in it
- What fundamentals to use to compare companies' assets including cash flow per share, net present value of reserves and book value per share
- How prospect generators grow by using other companies' money to advance projects and minimize risk
- Why over 60% of the world's exploration companies choose to list on the TSX–Venture Exchange and what you need to do to invest there
- The "annuity" advantage royalty companies offer and why exploration companies that possess them stand a greater chance for mineral discovery
- Understand the geopolitical risks of companies operating in foreign countries

- What is necessary in existing infrastructure for a mine to begin and sustain production
- Technology used to find, locate and gauge the size of a mineral deposit
- The differences between open pit and underground mining and what you need in each one to be profitable
- How to leverage your investments with warrants
- What to look for in a company's share structure that will give you the best chance of finding a stock that multiplies many times over
- Public relations programs and their influence over stock price
- The benefits and drawbacks of green field and brown field projects
- What makes an exploration company joint-venturing with larger companies a profitable strategy
- How to use ETFs to gauge market strength and money flow

This is just a macro view of *Junior Mining Investor,* but I believe it will set you on a path to greater profits through more consistent, educated trading.

The junior exploration and mining industry is one of the few sectors that offers life-changing investment returns. This doesn't mean it's easy to make money in speculative mining stocks. However, the more research and work you do, the better your chance to create great wealth. Investors must do their homework, call the companies regularly and be ready to execute positions when risk/reward dynamics are stacked in their favor.

There has never been a better time to invest in natural resources. Be a student of the markets and take advantage of the tremendous opportunity currently offered in junior mining and exploration stocks.

Kevin Corcoran
www.JuniorMiningInvestor.com

1

So You Think You Can Speculate?

Dr. Russell McDougal

Do you have what it takes to bring home mind numbing profits? Are you willing to venture into an investment arena where the risk reward ratio is so extreme that only the boldest survive and thrive? Do you realize that there are methods to stack the deck in your favor even when engaging in out and out speculation?

You would be wise to consider learning the art of speculation!

Yes, one can learn how to speculate successfully... just as I have done since 1993 in the field of natural resources exploration. The learning curve has been steep, and at times painful, yet there is no market on earth in which I'd rather participate. Where else can you readily double your money in a solid stock or bring home $5 ... $10 ... $20 ... or occasionally $30 for each initial dollar of investment? Of course, this isn't a one-way street and the risk of loss is also high. I will have much more to say in the near future as to exactly why I believe this field is a speculator's paradise. Warren Buffett said it best: "Pick a particular market niche, learn more about that sector than 90% of the other participants, and you will make your fortune." (Paraphrased)

We have entered into an era of global resource shortages, which isn't likely to be solved any time soon. The industrialization of China, India and Latin America is just one major factor underlying this trend. It is far superior to invest/speculate with the market currents in your favor. And now is a time that favors the market for natural resources. Let's look at just a few resource exploration stocks that have performed extraordinarily well over the last three to six years.

- Afriore Limited (AFO.TO) could have been purchased in July of 2004 for $0.29. It is currently (May 2007) trading at $8.72 primarily due to a platinum discovery in South Africa. Let's count that as 30X, and it still can go higher.

- Altius Minerals Ltd. (ALS.TO) could have been purchased in the spring of 2001 for $0.32. It is currently trading at $13.53 due to stellar management and uncanny deal making. That's a 40X return, but the wise are still holding shares for further appreciation.

- Silvercorp Metals Inc. (SVM.TO) could have been purchased for $0.35 in September of 2004, when it was then called SKN Resources. It now trades around $20 and has been higher still. They have a world class silver discovery in China. That's a 57X return with room to run.

Sure, it's easy to list some grand slam profits such as those I made with these particular choices, but it's much more difficult to pick the next big winners. That's exactly what I attempt to do on an ongoing basis. By knowing yourself and your chosen market, I am convinced you can stack the deck in your favor even when speculating. So let's delve into some of the methods of doing exactly that. First of all you must allocate carefully exactly how much you are willing to speculate. You should never speculate with money you are not willing to part with, especially when you initially enter such an arena. Neither should you risk money that would compromise your lifestyle should it find its way into the hands of others. And it is always better to pay off outsized debts than it is to risk money in search of outsized profits.

You must also decide the "eggs and the basket" issue. Is it ultra-risky to put all your eggs in one basket? If you decide, as I have, that it is actually best to put all the eggs (speculative funds only) in one basket, then you'd better watch that basket very closely! My "diversification" is simply through different elements and compounds being explored for, be they gold, silver, copper, oil, natural gas, uranium, molybdenum or fertilizers. It is a major task to understand and follow these similar stocks. Therefore, I cannot afford to get distracted by multiple other endeavors (biotech, medical, technology, etc.). It is humorous to me how many people speculate without even realizing it. Junk bonds are not the only thing deserving such a label, as more and more financial paper gets peddled to an unsuspecting public. Those that counted on their indefinite annual returns of 20% during the late 90's NASDAQ bubble have since learned the lesson that there are NO sure things. The same goes with all the real estate moguls who believed that real estate only goes up. The best speculations are ones taken intentionally!

You must also know yourself. Do you have the ideal temperament for putting significant amounts of money at risk in search of extraordinary gains? Can you sleep at night even though your bottom line got trimmed with a sharp instrument earlier in the day? Will you freak out if one of your holdings dips 20%, 50% or more? Do you get caught up in both mass euphoria and utter dismay and let it affect your portfolio decisions? Are you into 'momentum' or 'fad' investing and choose your positions accordingly? I will be presenting a series of articles on the art and skill of speculating in the resource exploration sector. Some of you may find you have this same calling.

There are some key rules to follow, with variations, when delving into resource exploration stocks. The most important one is to take total responsibility for your investment decisions and any subsequent consequences. You ultimately make buying and selling decisions, and you are the one who reaps the reward or pays the consequences. So take some money off the table when the market is kind to you, because it is often fickle. I would advise that you take the original money to safety once a stock doubles and then let the rest ride worry free. Some of the stock market mantras from the 90s are perfectly adaptable to resource investing. Once an ideal speculation is chosen you can "average down" or "hold for the long term". The idea is to get as many shares as you can as cheaply as you can. If the stock you have chosen after extraordinary due diligence plummets 30%, you need to be emotionally equipped to buy more instead of selling it.

Speculation is much like chess, bridge or golf . . . it is a life-long quest and will be mastered only by the disciplined and determined. It is an acquired skill and it can be a vocation or avocation. It is the narrow road, but it is frequently paved with GOLD.

Got a travel bag?

Since 1993, Dr. Russell McDougal has focused almost exclusively on gold, silver and resource investing. He has a particular affinity for silver and has studied virtually everything available on the topic since 1994. Rusty writes a weekly column for Investor's Daily Edge, an online investment newsletter. Sign up for your free subscription at www.InvestorsDailyEdge.com.

MINERALS OUR EXPLORATION COMPANIES SEEK

Au	**Gold**	money, jewelry, investment, coins, dentistry, electronics, aerospace
Ag	**Silver**	coins, jewelry, investment, tableware, photography, electronics, water purification
Pt	**Platinum**	jewelry, laboratory equipment, electrical contacts, automobile emissions control devices, spark plugs
Pd	**Palladium**	industrial catalysts, jewelry
Rh	**Rhodium**	alloying agent for hardening platinum and palladium, electrodes for aircraft, spark plugs, catalytic converters
U	**Uranium**	nuclear weapons, electricity generation, propulsion for nuclear ships and submarines
In	**Indium**	liquid crystal displays (LCD), indium phosphide semiconductors
Zn	**Zinc**	galvanizing steel, chemicals, sunscreen, alloyed with copper to make brass
Cu	**Copper**	plumbing, wiring, roofing, circuit boards, architecturals
Ni	**Nickel**	stainless steel, catalysts and other chemicals, foundry products, plating

Mo	**Molybdenum**	high temperature/strength stainless alloys including those used in oil and natural gas industry, flat panel TVs
W	**Tungsten**	used in tooling, to strengthen steel, mining equipment
Co	**Cobalt**	super alloys, parts in gas turbine aircraft engines, catalysts for petroleum and chemical industries
Fe	**Iron**	basic element in steel, castings, tenth most abundant element in universe
Mn	**Manganese**	used in steelmaking, aluminum alloys, fuel additive
Cr	**Chromium**	used in stainless steel for corrosion resistance, plating, anodizing
V	**Vanadium**	springs, axles, gears and other components, specialty stainless, e.g. surgical instruments
Ti	**Titanium**	lightweight, strong alloys, medical implants and devices, golf clubs
Al	**Aluminum**	aerospace alloys, transportation, construction, water treatment, cans and foil
Sn	**Tin**	corrosion coating on steel, canned food
Pb	**Lead**	lead-acid batteries, bullet and shot, solder, glass, fusible alloys

2

How to Pick a Good Mining Company

David Morgan

One of the most frequent questions I am asked is, "Where can I invest in precious metals to maximize returns?" The answer is not as straightforward as one might expect. As most who visit our website know, the mining equities have been in a bull market and I expect it will continue. There is still plenty of time for an investment in precious metals, but a wise investor should choose carefully ahead of the herd. Developing a mine involves an abundance of time and money. It can take five years or longer from the time a prospective property is identified until full production is achieved. Mills for the largest mines can cost an incredible amount of money. Think about it. Before exploration can take place, the ore body needs to be defined through a drilling program. Based on results, a feasibility study needs to be completed. Recently, this phase has taken on significant demands based upon current environmental concerns. At every step so far there is considerable risk.

EXPLORATION RISK

Not all exploration projects will lead to discovery. Many won't have enough of anything interesting that would generate share price gains.

ASSAY RISK

Some companies just release the 'good' assays. Salting a mine does occur. We only have to look at the Bre–X fiasco to know that drill results do not always "pan out". This is only part of the story though. For example, suppose you own a rich property, but do not have the financial capability to build a mine. You decide to sell your property. Now the prospective buyer uses a different lab to determine the value of the property and bids considerably less than what your results show. In other words, in some cases it is beneficial to skew the results depending upon which side of the transaction your interest is established.

MANAGEMENT RISK

Who's got a long-term track record of success? Who doesn't?

FINANCIAL RISK

Is the investment sound? How does it measure up against its peers? Is the bookkeeping accurate?

TRADING RISK

How liquid is your investment? Is there Institutional involvement? How many shares trade? How big is the spread between bid and ask? With many risks come potential rewards. Mining shares are leveraged to the price of the underlying asset gold or silver or both, for example. The higher the cost of mining, the greater the fluctuations in profits, and thus share price. Profit volatility can be illustrated. Consider the increase in earnings for two different gold mines.

Mine X has a mining cost of $200 per ounce.
Mine Y has a mining cost of $250 per ounce.

Now let us consider the increase in earnings if gold rises from $300 to $325 per ounce.

Company	Profit at $300	Profit at $325	Change
Mine X	$100	$125	25%
Mine Y	$50	$75	50%
Gold			8.3%

This example illustrates how a moderate increase in the price of gold can produce leverage of varying degrees for different mining companies. In this example, the higher cost producer shows increased leverage over the lower cost producer. This of course is only half the story.

What happens if the price of gold drops from $300 to $275?

Company	Profit at $300	Profit at $275	Change
Mine X	$100	$75	-25%
Mine Y	$50	$25	-50%
Gold			-8.3%

High cost mines mean high leverage plus high risk. There are other considerations. For example, how do you determine political risk? What about geographical risk? The topography and climatic conditions may determine when mining activity can take place and when it is impossible. Another factor in geographic risk is how many properties does a company own? If the company holds only one property, then the risk is greater than another company that holds several properties in different countries. My point is that determining the best investment areas for mining companies involves as much art as it does science.

QUALITY + SAFETY = MAXIMUM RESULTS

It is important to follow trends. If history is any guide, quality plus safety means maximum results. This has been our philosophy so far. The bigger, low debt, low hedged or lightly hedged companies have been favored over all others. This has proven to be a sound method. It does not mean that information on possible high flyers is avoided all together. But when smaller and less established companies are mentioned, it is the reader that is required to use discretion. Investors are tempted to apply standard investment analysis to mining companies. This does not work well. Right now a majority of mining companies do not allow for a price to earnings analysis to be performed. This type of analysis is more useful in trying to determine a market peak. Very few mining securities offer an income stream. There are some that do. But there are others who have tried and failed. Sunshine Mining Corporation had a silver-backed bond at one time.

IF IT IS NOT GROWN, IT HAS TO BE MINED

The mining business is tough, very tough. Yet mining is vitally important. As a member of the Northwest Mining Association, I am familiar with a slogan we have, "If it is not grown, it has to be mined". Think about that for a minute. I strongly believe that the entire financial complex is shifting from paper assets to tangible assets. It is not difficult to see that raw commodities always have value: food (agricultural commodities), clothing (cotton), transportation (oil), heating (natural gas), and shelter (lumber). Stock prices are based on many factors and influences. A company's earnings should play an important role. Unfortunately, the entire accounting profession and the numbers they produce, including earnings, are questionable. The shift is taking place and will continue for several years into the future.

Now back to mining stock analysis. A good method is to look at how much silver or gold you are buying per dollar invested. The math involved to find this answer is not really all that complicated. However, it never is an apple to apple comparison. Just because an investor has determined that company X has more ounces per dollar, does not make it a better buy. Some ore is easier to extract, some is easier to refine, other areas are easy to clean up and restore and others are not.

DIVERSIFICATION STILL TRIED AND TRUE

It is important to diversify in the metal area for several reasons. Any investor knows diversification is important and it applies to mining stocks as well. However, having lived through the first secular bull market in the metals, much of what I have written can be discounted by what I am about to write. The best market students study human nature because that is key to understanding how and why markets move.

A personal experience may help illustrate this better. The year was 1979 and many of the mining companies that I followed were exploding in price. I had a friend that was "late to the party" so to speak, but could not help but get caught up in the excitement. He had asked my opinion of various mining companies and I gave him some of my thoughts. I received a phone call from him about a month later, it was now 1980, he sounded very excited, yet a little relieved. I asked Phil what was going on.

"Well, you know what you said about choosing a mining company?" "Yes," I answered. "It just did not sound right to me, I looked at what you said, but so many of those companies had moved up so much. I finally found one on the American exchange and it was still around two bucks per share. It was named gold something. I bought it and four days later sold it for four dollars per share." "Great," I exclaimed. "Sorry, but I never heard of that company." Phil replied, "That is the craziest thing. They weren't a mining company at all. They just had gold in their name. Guess I sold it to someone else that thought it was a mining company too."

So the story goes. Phil was lucky. The point is that in a bull market people can get swept away with emotion. Phil's research was based upon a cheap stock that had gold in the name. We have experienced a similar situation with the dotcom stock issues. Fear and greed motivate people. In fact, they can motivate normally sane people to do something that they might not ordinarily consider. As an investor, it is most important to maximize your return while attempting to minimize risk as much as practical. There are several mining companies that offer ample opportunities for speculation. This is the case now. Near the end of the coming mining boom, there will be several times as many companies. This will be an indication that the investment cycle has run its course, but I do not expect to witness this for many more years.

David Morgan is the editor of the Silver Investor and publishes "The Morgan Report," a monthly newsletter focused on free market economics, precious metals and natural resource stock investing. Learn more about David and his investment philosophy at www.Silver-Investor.com.

3

Junior Gold Stocks

Scott Wright

There is no arguing that the gold-stock sector has been one of the hottest in the financial markets since the turn of the century. The venerable HUI gold-stock index has seen a nearly 1,000% rise from trough to peak in the last six years and the stocks that comprise it have won investors and speculators legendary gains. Within the gold-stock world though lies a sub-sector that is not represented by an index and really has no boundary on its potential. Like an underground blood sport event or a big city basement casino, junior gold stocks fly under the radar and only those investors who actively seek this realm may successfully enter it.

Drawing another analogy to the aforementioned locales, gambling in the junior gold-stock world can either leave you bloody and bruised with empty pockets or reward you with spectacular gains that even Las Vegas odds-makers could not fathom. Little known to the average investor, this gold-stock sub-sector supports capital markets that don't show up on most radars. These stocks are so petite that you'll never see mainstream media coverage on them nor will you likely get recommendations from your broker. But even with a limited pool of investors going after the junior gold stocks, their popularity has risen considerably in recent years. In and even out of the typical gold circles there has been significant chatter surrounding the up and coming junior gold stocks that are expected to shoot to the moon.

For investors seeking junior gold stocks in which to speculate, the primary challenge lies in not only identifying these stocks but in discerning which ones are the good ones. With hundreds of junior gold stocks to choose from, I decided to hunker down and seek out some of the quality junior gold companies that are positioning themselves to greatly capitalize on this gold bull going forward. I knew this task would be arduous, but I expected that the reward potential not only for my own trading capital but that of our loyal newsletter subscribers would be well worth it. So I spent the last few months threshing through hundreds of junior gold stocks in search of some high-probability-for-success winners. Sometimes this adventure seemed mind-numbing as it is often difficult to dissect these companies and peel away their layers in order to get a glimpse of their cores. But for the most part it was downright exciting. What an exhilarating experience it was to learn about the GenXers of the gold-mining industry!

Collectively, these junior golds hold the key to the future balance of the economics of gold. Whether directly or indirectly, junior golds will greatly contribute to the supply side of the gold trade. My intent for this first of a two-part commentary on this topic is to reveal some areas of research that I found most useful in analyzing junior gold stocks.

HISTORY/MANAGEMENT

When researching a junior gold stock, taking a close look at company history and its existing management team can be quite revealing. Those companies that are strong-suited in this area will advertise their prowess. But often you have to dig deep in such obscure resources as old prospectuses, regulatory filings, MDA reports, old press releases and perhaps even a refined online search. God bless the Internet! You will find that some juniors have rich histories that span through the flows and ebbs of a full commodities-market cycle. Yet others are fresh new start-ups that have emerged since today's secular gold bull took shape. And there are even a handful of others that may have gone through name and/or management changes to either mask the past or shift their strategic direction.

If there is a history, learn what you can from it and view it objectively. What accomplishments, if any, does a junior have on its resume? Has the company exhibited asset growth and valuation growth? What changes has it gone through and how has it weathered adverse market conditions? These are just a few of the questions that should be addressed in this line of research. Answers you may find when researching this thread will range considerably. Some juniors only ever want to explore for gold, and are good at it. It is not always a bad sign if a junior with a lengthy history has not yet graduated to become a gold producer. I found that some companies have outlined business plans that mandate a divestiture at the end of a gold project.

Some juniors are great at discovery but outright avoid development and hefty project-funding risks. They believe in increasing shareholder value by either keeping their gold in the ground or selling it to the bigger fish in order to obtain the capital to start the cycle all over again. For every encouraging story though there are those that are a bit shady. Some companies have been sitting on a project for decades without making significant progress. When the markets are tight they hibernate, and when the markets are good they turn on the spotlight steering unsuspecting investors to their stagnant stories.

As for management, experience is pivotal in the success of a junior. Junior gold companies have little room for error in their operations and an experienced management team with a successful background is of utmost importance. You will find that successful management teams are headed by highly trained geologists, experienced and respected industry tradesmen or a combination of the two. With company history, management history can be very telling when researching the junior golds. Have members of management had past successes or failures while in decision-making positions? Has the team or individual led successful voyages or captained sinking ships? Are the executives industry veterans or serial promoters?

Asking these questions and more will help lead to prudent decision-making. And the answers you find may astonish you. To give you an example, after a little digging, I discovered that some companies that looked good on the outside were actually founded or run by someone that drove previous resource expeditions into bankruptcy. Others were run by someone with a background in the tech industry with little knowledge of resource development. Probabilities for long-term success don't bode well for these types of companies. Good management and a productive history radically increase the odds that a junior can blossom in a gold bull market. Diligent research on this front can pay great dividends.

EXPLORATION

The title "junior gold" is synonymous with "junior explorer". This is because the essence of junior gold stocks is exploration. For the most part juniors do not produce gold. Their function in the lifecycle of bringing gold to market rests in discovery, advancement and development of promising gold deposits.

The juniors that we marvel at with hopes of massive gains usually possess a project or portfolio of gold projects that are in the exploration stage. And depending on the market capitalization of a junior, you can usually deduce in which phase it resides. An early phase of exploration in which many juniors reside is called greenfields. Greenfields exploration is the poke-and-find method of exploring a broad target area that has initially favorable geology with little or no evidence of mineralization. This is probably the most important phase of exploration in the gold industry as it is ultimately responsible for its longevity. Without greenfields exploration, global mined gold supply would dwindle in a matter of decades. And unfortunately, greenfields exploration is one of the riskier phases of exploration. The probability that an identified gold target turns out to be a mineable deposit is very low. And when various studies finally reveal a target to be a dud, then all the invested capital put into exploration ends up good-for-naught. Exploration is not cheap! Greenfields exploration is not only a vital stage for the juniors, but also the major producers. A lot of sunk capital goes into this phase. A sizable producer can absorb a greenfields failure, and actually plans for it since discovering gold is not the easiest thing in the world. But a junior that has very limited capital takes on far more leveraged risk in the greenfields phase. Many juniors become insolvent upon greenfields failure. This is a good reason why it is so vital that experienced geologists are on the payroll of the juniors.

Positive results from mapping, surface sampling and drilling in greenfields exploration could push a project to the next phase of exploration. This phase involves more detailed technical studies that include extensive drilling and core sampling. Many times an independent consultancy that qualifies under various mining codes performs these studies that are formally called scoping studies. A scoping study is usually the first step in examining the economic viability of a mineral deposit. If a scoping study returns positive results, then a project usually gets advanced to the feasibility phase. Feasibility studies many times begin with a less time- and capital-intensive pre-feasibility study. This study may provide reasonably accurate yet rough project cost and operating schedule projections. Mature miners with deeper pockets will sometimes use pre-feasibility studies to make a construction decision. Juniors don't usually have this luxury though because the bankers that finance the bulk of a junior gold project require what are called either full, bankable or definitive feasibility studies to be performed before they risk their capital on a gold mine that is slave to the volatility of the commodities markets.

These full feasibility studies are comprehensive technical reports compiled through extensive drilling programs that reveal the true depth and breadth of a gold deposit. This study typically provides detailed project capital costs, economic reserves, operating cost projections, mine life projections, IRR scenarios, recurring expenses, timelines and much more. Ultimately these phases don't have defined parameters and depending on the size of the deposit can have vastly different lead times. Some of the more extensive studies may take several years to complete especially for some of the thin-pocketed juniors that can't employ a dozen drills at a time. Now theoretically the more advanced an exploration project is, the higher the probability that deposit may come to life. This same logic can be used to scale market capitalization as hinted at above. But this line isn't always followed precisely, which is why each project needs to be examined independently.

After finding out where a junior gold stock falls in the exploration cycle, then you can start asking these questions. How long has it been in its given phase? Is it making progress in its efforts? Is it reporting its results and are they positive? Has it projected when the next phase will likely begin? In researching this thread you may come across some juniors that don't have as good a project as they claim. But you may also find some undiscovered and less-marketed juniors that have an undervalued project when scrubbed against their peers. Exploration activity should absolutely be considered when researching a junior gold stock.

RESOURCES

Resources are ultimately the bread and butter of a junior gold. In a nutshell, resources are the estimated gold ounces within a specific location that a junior claims to possess. This gold is identified through geologic evidence obtained via various methods and depending on the strength of the resource has an attached level of certainty relating to its economical extraction. All the wiggle words in this loose definition are important to note for resources. Whereas gold producers are extracting their gold from gold reserves that are proven to be economically feasible, resources are not yet so. Resources do not have enough evidence to presume economic viability. More testing and drilling needs to be performed in such feasibility tests, as mentioned above, in order for resources to get the upgrade to reserves. Though resources are the first step to defining a possible gold deposit, even the regulatory agencies that preside over the gold stocks require disclosures so as not to sway investors to believe that estimated resources will ever prove to be economical. Like when lifting a footprint at a crime scene, you can only estimate the size of the perpetrator. Until you have further evidence, nothing can be proved. This is the same reasoning for resources. Though resources are not yet proven to be economical, simply attaining resources through technical studies allows juniors to gain a foothold on their projects so that they may continue to advance exploration. And similar to the different phases of exploration, there are different levels of resources.

Resources scale up in viability with some of the standard phrases you will see being: Inferred, Indicated, Measured, Probable and Proven. Without getting too technical, the ore grade and sample size weigh heavily on which level a resource will fall in. Once enough evidence is obtained on the depth and breadth of a deposit, resources can scale up the resource curve either until the evidence supports shelving the project or taking it all the way to production.

And economics play a huge role in how these resources may be presented and viewed by the markets. It may be discovered that there are indeed resources within a deposit. But the geological intricacies of the deposit only allow these resources to be economically recoverable at $700 per ounce. Today these resources are not feasible reserves, but if gold is over say $1,000 per ounce a couple years from now, these resources will then become economically viable reserves. Again, resources need to be viewed objectively on a project-by-project basis. Some juniors have very strong resources and even reserves, and some have claimed really weak resources or none at all. Once you find out what type of a resource a junior has, then it is important to determine how its exploration will support and grow them. In examining junior golds, a red flag can be hoisted if no activity or operating plan is discernable for identified resources. A company that sits on its laurels and just hopes its resources alone will carry its stock through this gold bull will sorely disappoint investors.

The general rule of thumb for resources is the higher up the classification scale the better. Juniors that have a knack for discovery that results in identifying new resources as well as those juniors that grow and upgrade their existing resources should always be viewed with favor. In addition to the three research points I highlight above, there are two other major areas of focus I will discuss soon in part two of this junior gold stock commentary. First, funding and financing for the junior golds are often overlooked by many investors, but for a variety of reasons it is vital to pay careful attention to this area. Now more than ever geopolitics are playing an increasingly important role in the gold-mining industry. Juniors are certainly not immune to geopolitical travails. Stay tuned for part two of this series where I will dissect funding, financing and geopolitics pertaining to junior gold stocks.

Ultimately there are dozens of facets that need to be addressed in order to effectively research a junior gold stock before surrendering capital to this exciting sector. Before you entrust your hard-earned capital to a basket of junior gold stocks, useful research and analysis are crucial in order to uncover the true nature of a company. Junior gold stocks are fun and speculating in this realm can yield vast riches if played right. But it is important to look past the smoke and mirrors that many juniors exhibit. Though a company may look good from the outside and have good initial momentum, if it actually has poor assets without a legitimate business plan it will swallow investor capital so fast it would be difficult to recover.

The bottom line is junior gold stocks have the potential to reward speculators with legendary gains in this gold bull market. This risky class of gold-mining stocks is utilitarian in its existence as the juniors provide investors with vast speculative opportunities in addition to serving an important role in the gold mining cycle. And among the countless juniors to choose from there is a wide spectrum of quality that includes both the studs and the duds. But through diligent research it is possible to thresh out the good from the bad. With the three fundamental areas of focus I highlighted today along with two more that I will touch on in the next part of this series, we can possess the tools to help guide us to the winners.

Scott Wright publishes an acclaimed monthly newsletter, Zeal Intelligence, that details actual stock and options trades and provides in-depth market analysis and commentary. Zeal's goal is to build real world wealth through prudent trading. For weekly essays and more information visit www.ZealLLC.com.

4

12 Guidelines for Buying Gold Mining Stocks

Kenneth J. Gerbino

These twelve guidelines should help you better understand some investment basics regarding the mining industry, especially if you do not have a background in geology or mining engineering. I have kept this as non-technical as possible so no one falls asleep. Keep in mind, these are basic guidelines and far from complete.

1. If the company does not have an independent professional resource calculation for gold or silver or other minerals, know that someone is either speculating or guessing at the most critical data point regarding mining industry valuations. Be careful not to confuse "resources" with "reserves". Measured and Indicated resources are reliable as a resource. "Inferred resources" are very speculative mineral inventories, so be careful when "Inferred" is used. A resource still has a long way to go to become an economic deposit, as opposed to "reserves", which are deemed to be proven economic and mineable ounces calculated by very strict engineering and government rules. Canada's National Instrument 43–101[1] is one such guideline regarding resources and reserves.

---

[1] Shortly after the Bre–X scandal, the National Instrument 43–101 rule was developed by the Canadian Securities Administrators to standardize reporting of resources and reserves in a specific manner by a qualified person.

2. I would suggest your portfolio be 60% invested in companies already producing gold or silver profitably. The other 40% divide into companies close to production with impressive projects or very far along in defining large and significant mineral resources. Producers should include majors and mid-tiers (your monetary insurance, since they undoubtedly have the goods in the ground). Look for mid-tiers with good growth profiles. Junior producers with new projects are also okay. Companies with lots of money in the bank or access to sponsorship from top investment banks in Toronto, London and Vancouver is vital in this capital intensive business and always a good thing to look for. Diversify: have at least 15 good companies. Depending on your risk tolerance you could allocate a small portion to grass roots exploration stocks but know this is the very high-risk end of the business. The industry has changed in the last five years. Exploration and development budgets from 1998 to 2002 declined dramatically. Therefore going forward, in my opinion, any substantial project that is near feasibility (an extensive outside engineering report based usually on tens of millions of dollars of geological, metallurgical, and engineering work) could be a buy-out candidate for major and mid-tier companies that need to catch up on reserve replacement and growth.

3. "Good management" is an overused word. My definition of good management is 20-year mining professionals who have had successful executive positions with large or successful mining companies or projects in the past. If you see names like Barrick, Newmont, Placer, Anglo, Goldfields, etc., on the resume you are most likely dealing with some quality professionals. People who ran mid-tier companies or successfully helped bring medium to large projects to production also qualify. There are always exceptions, but you better know whom you are dealing with. Direct mail pieces

touting some gold stock and claiming top management should be carefully checked out.

4. Size is very important. The larger the deposit or potential resource the better. Small mines are not worth your trouble as there are few institutions that will finance them and fewer companies that will ever acquire them. With gold mines, try and look for 2–3 million ounces and above possibilities. Mining giant Goldfields, only targets projects with 2 million reserve ounces. With silver, 100 million ounces should be your minimum. But the above still has to be qualified. If the resource is too deep under the surface, of very low grade (richness), or has one of many other negative reasons, it may never be economical to mine. Tonnage is important. Big tonnage operations create economies of scale that can make some low metal values economic to mine. Three hundred million tonnes (a tonne is 2,204.62 pounds, not to be confused with a ton, which is 2,000 pounds) for an open pit gold mine is big. A ten million tonnes open pit is small. For an underground operation, tonnage can vary dramatically and grade and mining widths become more important (we will discuss this below), but one million tonnes would be small. For a base metal open pit deposit, one billion tonnes would be huge, while 20 million tonnes would be small. So remember in this business—Big is Beautiful.

5. Grade (richness) is crucial. How much bang for the buck are you getting per tonne of rock. If the grades are high enough the above tonnage discussion becomes less relevant. With a near surface potential open pit gold deposit, 2 grams per tonne (a gram is 0.03215 of an ounce) would be excellent. One gram would be fair as long as you don't have to remove too much waste rock to get at the ore. With underground mines, everything changes. Depth, the continuity and mining widths of the ore and the vertical or horizontal plane of the ore all come into play—as well as many other factors.

Generally, to be on the safe side, if you can find gold grades of 10 grams (about a third of an oz.) or more per tonne across mineralized sections averaging 3–4 meters or more in width, then you are looking at good potential. Lower grades across wider widths also work (i.e. 6–7 grams across 10 meters). Keep in mind these are rough guidelines and subject to many other factors, like depth, vein continuity, overall tonnage and much more. But the sweet spot in this industry is high grades across wide zones of mineralization.

6. Expansion possibilities for a company's production and resources/reserves are important. For non-producers, resource expansion is crucial, because as these companies drill and confirm more resources they will increase their intrinsic value. This helps them handle the big hurdles of either financing the mine or mines, selling-out, or bringing in a joint venture partner at reasonable terms. Mining companies with plenty of production and new mines coming on stream in the years ahead are usually a good group to own. Growth is good.

7. Cost per ounce of production is very important. Companies with high costs are more risky since a low metal price market will make them unprofitable, but they will have considerable positive leverage if metal prices go up. A gold mine with a $325 cost per ounce, doesn't make much at $375 gold, but if gold goes to $425, the mining profit doubles. High cost producers are like a double-edged sword. I like low cost producers. They are safer, have lots of cash flow to buy new properties and mines, will have more funds for exploration and development and could eventually pay strong dividends if gold stays in a new high price range over the years (i.e. $450–500). Also large mining companies are not going to buy-out high cost producers. They are risky and migraine headaches for management. Mining costs are mostly a function of grades, mining widths and tonnage. If you can talk to

a mining engineer and get a handle on the cost per oz. or tonne of the operation, you are acquiring crucial data for your analysis. Companies operating at high costs (within $100 of the gold price) or that have projects that look like they will be high cost producers, should be avoided. High costs equal high anxiety.

8. Value per ounce: How much you are paying for the gold in the ground is an important stat. The lower the better. The following guidelines relate to a $350–400 gold price. If gold were to go higher, these numbers would increase. For advanced exploration companies, try and stay in a valuation range around $15 per ounce of resource in the ground. As an example, a company with 15 million shares outstanding selling for $5 per share has a $75 million market cap. With a 5 million ounce resource, the market capitalization per ounce is $15. As companies move up the food chain and expand and define the resource and test metallurgy and do engineering studies, the market capitalization per ounce should go up to $30–50 per ounce. Depending on the quality of the deposit these valuations can change. Producing companies, if bought out, can go for $100 to $150 per ounce of "reserves" in the ground. That is an important guideline. You do not want to buy a stock where you are already paying $100 per ounce for just a "resource" (which means the "reserve" will actually be lower). With the company just in the advanced exploration stage, there won't be enough upside unless the deposit gets a lot larger. Advanced developmental (meaning feasibility to actual construction) companies can be bought out for $40–75 per ounce of resource or much more depending on many factors that are beyond the scope of this writing. Usually the value of the ounces and the stock price go up as more and more confidence is gained in the project. Initial resource definition usually allows for a value of $5–10 per ounce. At the bankable feasibility stage those same ounces could be valued at $40–75 per ounce. If you see a mining company

with a well defined resource and the gold ounces are valued at only $5 per ounce or so, just know there is probably a reason and it is probably bad. Most likely those ounces will never see daylight due to any number of reasons: environmental, logistics and infrastructure problems, political risk, low grades, high capital costs, narrow mining widths, high strip ratios (how much waste rock has to be removed to get to the ore in an open pit operation) and a host of other reasons. There is a right price for the ounces, don't overpay.

9. In a favorable gold mining environment, which I believe we will have for the next 10 years, it doesn't pay to take undue risks. Try and find good merchandise and be careful of the small grass roots exploration companies. Surface sampling is the key to the difficult exploration business. Positive soil and loose rock samples on a prospective property may have come from many miles away twenty million years ago. This means an ore body that is hopefully under the ground is not there. Only one inch of geological movement in a subsurface rock structure every 100 years equals in 20 million years, 3.2 miles. In geology you are dealing with billions of years. Mountains you see were once ocean floors, etc. Large and extensive outcrops (surface rock formations) that have mineral showings can be a good indicator as well as widespread crude and small local native mining activity. But it is no easy task finding these minerals in large enough deposits to be economic to mine. Surface showings are actually very important indicators for economic mineral discoveries but unfortunately they are still high-risk speculations.

10. A key stat is cash flow per share if the company is already a producer. Large gold mining companies can sell for 15–20 times cash flow in a good gold market. Mid-tier and smaller producers can sell for 25–35 times current cash flow because of expected cash flow increases, from new mines coming on stream. In this case the market is anticipating the future.

Beware high cost producers selling at high multiples of cash flow, as they will get hit very hard if gold has a set back. Companies expecting cash flow from future projects are usually valued using a net present value criterion. In this method the entire future cash flow of a mine is laid out and a value is placed on this cash stream, taking into consideration the time value of money. How much is the $500 million dollars that the mine will make in the years 2008 through 2018 worth today in the present. The future cash flows have to be discounted in order to arrive at some sort of present value for the projects. Many times a 5–10% discount rate is used. I believe a lower discount rate is also okay, since gold is an anti-discounting currency (i.e. gold's price should go up with inflation and interest rates therefore negating the discount rate because it will keep it's future purchasing value). Earnings-per-share is a tricky stat for the miners because of so many non-cash charges and accounting complexities. In the long run it all comes out in the wash, but during the years of the life of a producing mine, cash flow is the king. Look hard at cash flow per share or expected cash flow from projects.

11. Comparables are very important. Why would you buy a stock where for every $1 you invest you get $5 of gold in the ground when another company with very similar fundamentals and resources gives you $40 of gold in the ground for every $1 you invest? There actually may be a good reason, but the point is you should know what that reason is. Comparisons are an important ingredient to avoid overpriced companies and missing some real bargains. We constantly do comparables at Kenneth J. Gerbino & Co. and I suggest you do also. One should compare the basics: grades, tonnage, costs per ounce, costs per tonne, smelter charges (for base metal deposits), reserve or resource value per dollar invested, market cap per reserve/resource ounce, discounted cash flows and the net present values of the mining assets. Comparables allow you to better shop the market.

12. Be careful of the term "gross metal value." This is all the precious metal ounces or base metal pounds in the ground multiplied by the current price of the metals. It is misleading unless you have a lot more information and knowledge. Just know that with any mineral deposit a company will never recoup anything near the gross metal value of what is in the ground. The ore will have a mine waste factor (5–15%), recovery losses in the mill or from the leach pads (5–20%), and smelter, refinery, transportation and penalty costs for base metals (20–35%). Throw in royalties, state and local taxes and other expenses and you will see that gross metal value is less important to your analysis than all the other ingredients that would determine a quality mining investment. It doesn't mean the term is useless but it can be dangerous to use on its own.

Well, there you have some basic guidelines that I hope will help you through all the press releases and some of the direct mail hoopla about all the billion dollar mountains out there. Remember the more homework you do the better off you'll be. Good luck in what looks like a long-term, mostly bullish precious and base metals market.

Ken Gerbino heads Kenneth J. Gerbino & Company. The company manages private equity accounts as well as the Gerbino Gold Group, LLC, a private fund that invests in precious metals mining stocks. For more information please visit www.KenGerbino.com.

5

Junior Gold Stocks 2

Scott Wright

As this gold bull market continues in its secular uptrend, gold stocks have become increasingly popular as their gains are greatly leveraging those of their underlying metal. And within this hottest-of-the-markets stock sector, a sub-sector has emerged that investors have embraced and adored. Junior gold stocks tend to thrive in gold bulls, and as this particular bull heats up, more and more investors are looking for a venue in which to entrust their speculative capital. Junior golds lie in an adrenaline and risk-laden sub-sector that can sure take investors on a wild ride. And picking winners in these small market cap stocks can yield monstrous gains. But unless you have countless hours of free time to research the junior golds, it is often difficult for the average investor to know where to start to discover some high-probability-for-success winners.

Over the last few months, I've spent quite a bit of time re-searching junior golds and found some very useful areas of research that all investors should consider before they speculate in this gold-mining class. I have refined these important areas of research into five major sections. Each of these sections can reveal a wealth of information that should help guide the decision-making process of which juniors in which to invest. With a little diligence, any motivated investor can use these threads of research and apply them to any junior gold stock they choose. In the first part of this commentary, I dove into the importance of looking into a junior's history/management, exploration and resources. Strength in each of these areas is vital for the success of a junior gold stock as are these next couple sections that focus on the importance of geopolitics and financing/funding.

GEOPOLITICS

Geopolitics is always a key component to consider before investing in any resources company. This is especially important for gold due to the growing scarcity of historically safe gold mining venues. Today more than ever gold miners are forced to scour the far corners of the planet in order to discover the gold deposits of the future. Unfortunately, a sizeable portion of the untapped global gold resources, grace some not-so-popular regions of the world. And in order to supply the future demand for the Ancient Metal of Kings, the gold industry must increasingly deal with corrupt governments, cultural challenges and logistical nightmares.

In first world, free-market, gold-producing countries such as Canada, Australia and the U.S., as well as Marxist-led gold-rich South Africa, it has become increasingly difficult for junior explorers to stake fresh and exciting claims. Because of this, many juniors are forced to venture into relatively untapped countries that host varying degrees of geopolitical sensitivities. Some of the best junior gold companies are finding gold in the countries of war-torn central Africa, socialist-swinging Latin America and previously untouchable Asia including China, Mongolia and the former Soviet Union republics. And depending on the primary country of operation, geopolitical-risk discounts must be considered for many junior gold stocks. With the strength of our current gold bull and the push for global discovery, this discount has somewhat increased in recent years. Regardless of the political state of a country, governments are not blind to the fact that the world economy is in the midst of a major commodities bull market. Fortunately many countries recognize that they cannot exploit and profit from their natural resources without the injection of foreign capital and expertise, thus they're respecting free markets and opening their arms to foreign investment.

But on the flip side of this coin, there are those governments that are repulsed by the thought of foreigners profiting within their borders. As seen in recent years, many countries have taken to over-taxing and in some cases nationalizing resources that foreign companies are developing or mining. And then there are those countries that are under-governed with the federal bodies having little control over the affairs within their borders. As a libertarian this style of government is appealing, but in non-first-world countries this usually equates to safety hazards. The threat of violence, war and terror supports further discounts to junior golds operating within countries plagued with this risk.

Most of the junior golds we look at are North America-based companies, hence their trading locale. And those juniors doing business in geopolitically-unstable countries are some-times finding it very difficult to garner local support and/or obtain governmental permitting for a project that would likely greatly help the respective economy. Geopolitical risks can sometimes bear heavy costs to cash-strapped juniors. When researching any junior gold stock it is imperative to weigh geopolitical risk. The country of operation needs to be strategi-cally examined and its history and reputation with foreign business and its dealings with resource-specific companies should be considered. Sometimes the high-risk projects are valued accordingly but sometimes they are well undervalued and speculative opportunities may be available.

There are excellent junior golds that are trying to operate in such geopolitically-risky countries as Venezuela, China and the Congo that have projects valued at just a tenth of what they would be if they were operating in a safe domicile. If these projects move forward and garner support, obtain the necessary permitting and eventually pour gold, it could mean vast riches for those investors who believed in their stories and accepted their geopolitical risks. But it is of utmost importance to remember that geopolitical risk is usually out of the control of the juniors. These juniors can indeed greatly reward you if all turns out as planned, but it is important to stay aware of any threatening situations. A project can just as easily turn for the worse as it can for the better.

FINANCING/FUNDING

All junior gold stocks typically have one thing in common, the constant challenge of financing. The continuous struggle of obtaining, retaining and maintaining working capital for operations weighs heavily on the success of a junior gold. Unlike producers that are able to generate cash flows from the sale of their metals, pure explorers do not have a recurring source of revenue to draw upon. The primary source of capital for junior golds in the exploration stage comes from equity financing and equity financing is a fascinating fixture within the junior gold world. But this form of financing is wrapped with intricacies that are important for a prospective investor to understand, because depending on how these financings are structured, they could eventually make or break a junior. Now in order to maximize capital from both initial offerings and subsequent stock sales, a junior needs to build on a strong foundation that effectively tells its story. Juniors need to have the same mentality as a televangelist. The more believers a televangelist can convert the better his cash flow to support future ministries. Juniors need to gain believers in their story too in order to obtain enough capital to keep them functioning. This is why the marketing and promotional games commonly associated with the juniors are so important. But there is a fine line these companies walk in order to balance the strength of a story and their need for capital. When researching juniors it is important to look past the smoke and mirrors that their first-look facades may present.

The reason investors need to err on the side of caution when it comes to financing is due to the unfortunate and pestilent presence of serial promoters. Some juniors may be guilty of over-promoting their assets while others are guilty of misleading investors by telling a story that is downright false in order to inflate their stock prices. Researching this thread serves a dual purpose. First, it forces you to utilize other aspects of research that include history, management, exploration, resources, and geopolitics to determine the strength and legitimacy of the story a junior is trying to tell. The second lies on the other side of the line where you may come across a junior that is poorly marketed and not spreading its story well enough. In this case diligent research could prove to present a great buying opportunity.

Regardless of its promotional prowess, the interest in and demand for a junior gold stock ultimately contributes to the amount of capital it will receive through equity financing. It is also important to keep an eye on the structure and volume of any private placement(s) a junior may be party to. A typical junior-level private placement of shares, especially from the release of shelved shares after the company is public, consists of a consortium of investors that subscribe to shares and/or warrants at a fixed price. In many cases some of the investors in a private placement are indeed the firms or individuals tasked to market and promote the stock.

This is acceptable, but be leery of aggressive marketing campaigns that might correspond with the timing of the unlocking of restricted shares. Don't buy on hype, but on unbiased and intelligent research. Once financing is procured it is then prudent to find out where the money is going. A good junior should be using the lion's share of its financing for exploration with a small and reasonable balance for other expenses such as compensation and marketing. This information is easily obtainable within the public filings of their financial statements. Another thing to look at for the capital-challenged juniors, falls in the project funding game. If a junior is strong enough so its equity financings can take it all the way to the final feasibility phase of a gold project, then it must begin to consider obtaining the funds to actually construct a gold mine. The small minority of juniors that actually make it to this point find that the capital costs required to construct a gold mine usually dwarf the costs of exploration. This is one reason why many juniors that get to this phase will either joint venture their projects to a senior partner that can manage the funding or just outright sell them to the highest bidders. In reality, very few juniors actually construct and operate a gold mine.

Constructing a gold mine can cost from the tens of millions on the low end up to well over a billion dollars on the high end. With most junior gold stocks having market caps well under $1 billion with very limited working capital, equity financings are often not enough. So if positive feasibility tests give the green light for mine construction, these juniors need to muster up some serious capital to move forward. This capital usually comes in the form of debt financing.

For those mature juniors that are taking the path toward gold production, project funding is an area that needs to be closely examined. Once the tedious technical studies and environmental permitting are complete, large international banks are usually called upon to provide debt facilities that allow the juniors to construct a mine. And because these banks are lending money to small companies with no collateral that do their business in a sector that is highly volatile and at the mercy of the markets, a lot of intricacies are packaged into the loan requirements. Quite unfortunate for the junior gold explorers but in most cases necessary through the eyes of the bankers to partially protect their money; some variant of hedging is likely to find its way into the loan requirements. There are different ways a hedging facility can be structured, but the most common is in the form of forward sales. Forward sales are exactly what they sound like, selling forward a portion of future gold production at a fixed price. It is very difficult to find an early-stage gold producer that is not slave to hedging. In a bear market, hedging was the smart bet for many miners. But in a bull market, hedging can really hurt profits for many years until the obligation is either met or restructured. Imagine being locked in to selling gold for $400 per ounce while the open market is paying hundreds of dollars per ounce higher, ouch! So though hedging seems like a necessary evil for some of these small companies to bootstrap their way to future success, it is still prudent to examine the details of any hedging arrangement.

When examining a hedging structure, a heavy hedge can indeed be a showstopper in the speculation decision. I like to look at junior hedging arrangements as a portion of their total gold reserves. If too high of a percentage of gold is sold forward, then it is not worth risking your capital in a company where a bull market would eat it alive. But if the hedge appears like it will not be too heavy a burden in the future and rests on a minority of the gold reserves, the junior might be worth the risk. Each situation should be examined independently.

CONCLUSION

History/management, exploration, resources, geopolitics and financing/funding should all be viewed objectively. Each of these areas of research can be weighted differently depending on the junior gold stock in question. Depending on the size and stage of a junior some of these areas may not be applicable. And believe it or not junior gold risk usually scales with size. Though not always the case, the larger the junior the less risky it should be. In my eyes there are four different levels juniors can fall into. The largest and most mature juniors are on the verge of becoming gold producers. These juniors have completed advanced studies on their gold projects and are about to or have started construction of a gold mine. For these strong juniors gold production is imminent within the next 24 or so months.

The next level junior hovers around the mid-tier level. This company has resources through preliminary positive technical studies and has a defined drilling program to advance its project(s). Within the next 12 to 24 months this company expects to make an economic viability decision on its flagship project. The next level junior a good friend of mine has coined as the "nano-junior." This junior is on the very small side of the scale as far as valuation goes yet has promise looking forward. This company could be just getting started in the resource development game and has land holdings that are "promising" with very early testing showing encouraging results.

The last level junior I have dubbed the "dot-junior." This junior, like some of the infamous dot-commers of the tech bubble, is a trend chaser, a serial promoter or a schemer. It typically spends more money on marketing, promotion and salaries than it does on exploration. And its sole purpose is to exploit the gold bull and shamelessly suck in some of the capital that junior gold stocks command. The dot-junior has no desire to ever become a gold miner, yet can be stealthily disguised with a pretty website and fancy "market speak." Beware of the dot-juniors.

Are the juniors you are looking at poised to blossom in this gold bull market? A company doomed for failure may have good initial momentum as it follows the industry trend, but when it's revealed that it has poor assets without a legitimate business plan, watch out. The bottom line is due diligence is essential for successful stock picking. And for the junior golds it is even more important as this riskiest class of mining stocks has very little coverage outside of juniors' self-directed marketing and promotional campaigns. Any investor can use the research tools I highlighted above and apply them to any junior.

As this secular gold bull matures and continues to gain more popularity, a larger pool of capital from mainstream investors should greatly bid up the gold stocks. And among the gold stocks, the juniors should really thrive as their exploration projects stand to greatly influence the future of the gold industry.

6

How to Choose a Uranium Stock: Ten Tips Investors Should Know

Kevin Bambrough and Jean Francois Tardif

1. One of the best indicators of a project's potential success could be past ownership. It's best to try to buy any mining stock early in the cycle. Try to pick up properties that were worked by majors during the last bull market but which eventually dropped during the lows of the bear market. During the last uranium boom of the 1970s, many majors decided to completely exit the uranium sector.

2. Study the value of ore body with regards to its value per tonne, or its recoverable metal. Estimate the "all in" costs and feel comfortable with what you are paying. Risks-to-reward doesn't favor pure exploration. Typically, we avoid pure exploration plays unless management is excellent, they have a large prospective land package and the company is well financed.

3. Look for good, proven management, which has been successful in the past.

4. Look for solid shareholders. It is always nice to see that management has a large stake in the company. Often, this makes them value their paper more, and they will be less likely to engage in reckless stock issuance. If not management, I get comfort seeing that successful fund managers have large holdings. It is even better to see that a major company in a related industry has taken an interest in the company.

5. Look at the property's infrastructure. Find out about electricity and water costs required for exploration, development and production. Find out about roads, rail, trucking, access and proximity to a mill.

6. Look for hidden value in the company. We always consider the value of existing infrastructure. From time to time we have been able to buy companies where existing facilities, perhaps a mill or shafts more than justify the entire market cap of the company. Past drilling for uranium will save money. Some companies have properties with very expensive shafts and/or mills. There are also companies with large extensive databases like Energy Metals Corporation (TSX: EMC) and Strathmore Minerals (TSX: STM). These databases of past drilling on various properties can be used to continue to acquire good prospects and help sell pieces of land. I would expect that they would also be able to use the data to farm in on other properties or sell other property owners' valuable drill-hole data.

7. Buy emerging stories. It is great to find a company before it has any analyst coverage or even covered by letter writers.

8. Find out if the property is in a pro-mining environment. Ultimately, you need to mine. It's best to have a property in a location where government is pro-mining. We will still invest, though, as long as this factor is discounted in the stock. Some countries are so hungry for investment they will offer

favorable tax rates and other incentives. Permitting can be costly and take a long time so this is very important.

9. Study the capital costs for the project and the currency in the country where the project is located. Typically, the lower the capital costs, the less risk in the project. The less a company risks in time and money to find out if a mine is economical, the greater its chance of success. Larger capital-intensive projects usually take longer to bring on, and you could risk missing an important part of the cycle. I also like to consider currency moves and their possible impact. A strengthening local currency can drive up costs and destroy margins. A falling currency can dramatically improve the economics of the project.

10. Funding can improve the story or outlook. Make your cash work. It's not really an option for a small investor but as an institution we love to invest in companies when we think our cash is going to make a huge difference. Examples include when Aflease (now SXR Uranium One–TSE: SXR) had cash problems and was being deeply discounted, or our recent Tournigan (TSX: TVC) funding to pay for confirmation drilling and exploration on the Jahodna uranium deposit in Slovakia.

This list was compiled by Kevin Bambrough and Jean Francois Tardif of Sprott Asset Management and is presented on www.StockInterview.com, a news provider focused on uranium, coal-bed methane, molybdenum and various specialty stories that play a role in the world's energy markets.

7

How to Minimize Risk in Speculative Gold and Resource Stocks

Adrian Day

There is no doubt that gold and resource stocks are high flying, with the sector outperforming stocks and bonds for the last several years. The stocks, never fundamentally "cheap," have been trading at high-tech style multiples. But these stocks are traditionally very volatile, and the risk, also very high. This is true both on a long-term and short-term basis. Many thinly traded exploration stocks can move 10% or more in a single day, while even the leaders in the sector can experience extraordinary declines when the market turns, even temporarily.

The XAU is the index of the largest global gold and silver stocks. In a single month in 2006 (May 5th to June 8th) the index fell over 20%. That was on a short-term drop in the price of gold. On a longer-term basis, the declines can be even more dramatic; the index fell almost 60% in the 18 months following the peak in mid-1996. That was a relentless, week-by-week decline, interrupted by only a few minor blips. And the juniors fell more, of course, with declines of 80%, 90% and even more quite common. Many went bankrupt.

So what's the more cautious investor to do? We will start by assuming that the gold and resource market has further to go.

This is not the place for that argument. But it should be clearly understood that if the gold price has peaked and drops over the next year or two, it will be extremely difficult for any investor in the sector to make money. At the minimum, he will be swimming against the tide. Conversely, in a strong market, the broad mass of stocks in the sector, tend to go up to some extent or another. As the old saw has it, "a rising tide lifts all boats." Success in investing can be attributed to three important, if not equal, factors: the broad market, stock selection, and management techniques.

WAYS TO MINIMIZE RISK IN A GOLD PORTFOLIO

So let's stipulate that the broad trend is on our side, and gold and resources continue in a bull market. Management techniques are very important to success, and more cautious investors can minimize their risk by employing sensible tactics. This includes everything from using limit orders, being patient and buying on dips, not chasing prices, selling (perhaps part of a position) after an extraordinary run up in stock price, cutting losses quickly when a story changes, avoiding margin, and most of all, maintaining some semblance of balance in the portfolio. These somewhat prosaic exercises require time and knowledge, but they can mean the difference between mediocre and exceptional success over the longer term.

We should also make clear that different investors have different reasons for owning gold at different times. It may be purchased purely as insurance protection or portfolio diversification. Or perhaps one is buying gold and resource stocks in order to gain exposure to assets that one believes are in a long-term bull market. The kind of securities one buys, and the management of these securities, should be different for different objectives. For insurance protection, for example, one should purchase assets that have the most direct relationship with gold itself and as little possibility of risk, other than the risk in the gold price itself. Thus, for insurance, gold bullion, or bullion coins, are the most effective asset, while gold Exchange Traded Funds (such as GLD: NYSE), which mirror the price of gold, are also suitable.

A more conservative investor, and one who does not want to be trading a lot, can gain exposure to the long-term bull market, by buying the largest, more diversified and most solid of the blue chips and simply holding them. Here, one should emphasize companies with strong balance sheets, a large diversified asset base and low costs. In gold, for example, this might include Newmont Mining (with a strong asset base); Goldcorp (low costs); Meridian (strong balance sheet and low costs, though little diversification in assets); and South Africa's Gold Fields (with strong assets). At any given time, one or more of these will go through periods of underperformance, but over time— assuming a bull market, it is most likely that a simple portfolio of the biggest and best, held for the duration, will give solid returns.

WHY MOST EXPLORATION COMPANIES NEVER MAKE MONEY

More active investors, of course, venture down the good chain, to small producing or development companies, or even exploration companies. Such stocks can provide the most leverage and the biggest gains, but they also inherently have the highest risk. How does one minimize the risk in this sector? Apart from lots of homework, some expertise, the right temperament, and sensible portfolio management, the best way to minimize risk, while maintaining exposure to the upside that comes with discovery, is by selecting companies that themselves have a risk minimization business model.

The traditional model for an exploration company is straightforward. A geologist finds a property that he believes may have promise. He and his team raise money on the back of that project. The money is put in the ground in exploration and drilling to prove up the property (this is assuming it's not wasted on expensive dinners and promotion). Sooner or later the money runs out and the company has to go back to the market for more money. If there has been some early success, they may be able to raise more money at a reasonable price. If there has been little success, then raising more money to continue exploration will either be very expensive (high dilution) or near impossible.

Given that most exploration targets never give birth to a discovery, and fewer still ever become revenue-producing mines (forget about how many mines ever earn a positive return on their capital), then it becomes very clear very quickly why this traditional model is a long-odds gamble, however diligent the company management, or however prospective the property might appear. Why then do so many companies follow this model? Overconfidence and the promise of riches! If one owns a property and can prove up a discovery, then the leverage is enormous. But the risk of failure, or at best, constant dilution, is too great.

LOW-RISK BUSINESS MODELS ARE A SURER WAY TO SUCCESS

There are better ways. Two basic business models minimize risk, and both involve using other people's money to explore and develop properties. The first is the royalty model. This involves purchasing existing underlying royalties on properties (or creating royalties for exploration companies that need financing). Royalties give the royalty holder rights to certain income from the mines. They come in various forms (gross revenue or net smelter, meaning a percentage of the revenue; or net profits, meaning a percentage of a mine's profits after all expenses). They can be at a fixed rate, or more frequently at a sliding scale, which varies with the price of the underlying commodity.

The second model is that of a prospect generator. This involves looking for properties with potential, but spending as little as possible in the early stage before bringing in a partner to spend the exploration dollars. Of course, by bringing in a partner, one gives up part of the potential, but can spread one's risk; it's a little like having 30% of a dozen lottery tickets instead of all of just one. The odds of success increase dramatically, while just as importantly, the risk of total failure is dramatically diminished.

In both models, one is essentially using other people's money for the risky part of the business, gaining more certain exposure and less risk at the cost of less leverage (and leverage can be a two-edged sword, as we know). This is not to say that these two business models do not have any risk; of course not. If the price of the underlying commodity declines, the value of these companies as well as the market perception will decline. Similarly, a mine may not make any money and a net profits royalty may never pay out a dime, or an exploration program (albeit one that someone else is financing) may not find anything of value. The key, however, is that one's own expenditures are clearly defined and limited and the company is not responsible for overruns and problems, nor any liabilities associated with the mine. The stocks of companies with these low-risk models may not necessarily have the strongest performance over the shortest time frame, but they do have the lowest risk over time and will participate in a strong bull market.

WHY ROYALTIES ARE SUCH A GOOD BUSINESS

Let's look in a little more detail at the benefits of owning royalties on mines instead of doing the mining. A gross revenue and NSR royalty are the purest forms of royalty, and once purchased, there is no further risk or liability. One sits back and collects the checks, whether the mine operator is making money or not. Unlike holding a working interest in a mine, the royalty owner is not responsible for any share of the capital costs, nor responsible for fixing any problems that are a daily part of the mining business. Royalties are very high margin businesses, and administrative costs can be kept to a minimum. It is like owning an annuity, but one where the value and revenue go up if the price of the underlying commodity increases. Not for nothing does

Warren Buffett, chairman of Berkshire Hathaway, say that "the best business is a royalty on the growth of others."

There are two main royalty companies at present: Royal Gold (RGLD: NASDAQ) by far the larger, and the newer International Royalty (ROY: AMEX). Royal Gold has fewer but larger royalties, all in the precious metals arena. International Royalty holds over 60 royalties in a broad range of commodities (from nickel to uranium and coal), most of which are not currently producing.

A DIFFERENT MODEL FOR EXPLORERS

The prospect generator takes a different approach to minimizing risk, one that typically requires less capital, but where management is arguably more critical, both in finding early stage properties that appear to hold potential and in negotiating for partners (trying to give away as little as possible in exchange for a greater expenditure). In this approach, typically a company will spend little on initial exploration, taking properties to the point where they may be attractive for partners, and then brings in a partner who may spend all the exploration dollars up to the point of a feasibility study prior to a production decision, in exchange for earning into the property, in stage, up to 70%. The beauty is that the prospect generator can preserve its own capital to find more properties and do the same over again, building up a portfolio to diversify risk and increase the chances of being part of a discovery.

Prospect generators typically like to have a few different partners, both senior and junior companies. Seniors as partners can increase credibility, but since they have higher thresholds, they often back out of ventures if they do not appear large enough, even if there has been some success. They also tend to be more bureaucratic, making the prospect generator subject to the larger company's priorities. On the other hand, they usually have the capital required to be aggressive should developments warrant. There are numerous prospect generators in the market.

Management and track records are important factors to consider as well as the property portfolio and balance sheet. Some leading companies include:

- Virginia Mines (VGQ: TSX): top management, very strong balance sheet; a broad portfolio of active projects in various minerals and with various partners, all in Quebec. Virginia is the archetype of this business model, following its successful discovery of the Eleonore deposit, subsequently sold to Goldcorp.

- Rimfire Minerals (RFM: TSX): focusing on Canada, Alaska and Nevada, with several projects, mostly gold.

- Miranda Gold (MAD: TSX): focus on gold in Nevada, utilizing several partners.

- Almaden Minerals (AAU: AMEX) has numerous copper and gold projects in Canada and Mexico, and several active ventures, mostly with junior companies.

- Lara Exploration (LRA: TSX) is taking the prospect generator model to Brazil, with a handful of projects (in gold and tin), and a large portfolio for the explored and ventured.

VARIATIONS OF A THEME

There are also some companies with somewhat different business approaches to the pure prospect generator, but have intended to minimize risk and use other people's money where possible. First, we might mention that Newmont Mining (NEM: NYSE), the world's second-largest gold mining company, has a very successful division which both owns royalties and joint ventures grass roots properties; this is Newmont Capital, and although it consistently contributes solid cash flow to Newmont, it is only a small part of the entire company.

Silver Wheaton (SLW: NYSE) has taken an innovative approach by purchasing the silver streams from diversified mines. Most silver mined today is a byproduct of other metals in a larger mine (either gold or zinc or tin and so on). The tin miner sees the silver he produces as a way of minimizing his costs, but is not particularly interested in the potential of silver. So Silver Wheaton has acquired rights to the silver streams (the revenue attributable to the silver production) in exchange for an upfront payment followed by a fixed cost per ounce. For the seller, the benefit is clear: it gets cash up front, and is guaranteed a fixed revenue for its silver production, which, after all, is simply a byproduct. For the buyer, Silver Wheaton, the benefit is also clear: in exchange for an upfront payment and a fixed cost per ounce, it receives all the upside from higher silver prices. It becomes, therefore, a pure silver company (pure companies tend to command higher multiples in the market), and as with a royalty company, is not responsible for any problems or liabilities at the mine.

Vista Gold (VGZ: AMEX) accumulated gold resources at low cost during the down years with no intention of mining itself. Mining of course is where the greatest risks occur; it is often said that Murphy works overtime in the mining business. Instead of mining itself, Vista looks to maximize value by doing the exploration or development work necessary to bring resources up to modern reserve standards, and aims to dress the properties up to attract partners or even sell them. It has a dozen properties around the world at various stages of development, equivalent to about 0.4 ounce of gold per share. It is like holding a permanent call on gold, with minimal carrying costs.

Altius Minerals (ALS: TSX) started as a plain-vanilla prospect generator in Newfoundland, but has emerged into a large, diversified company by taking an innovative approach to leveraging its skills, generating projects that it can sell to others and retain an interest. We'll look at Altius and another of these companies, Virginia, in more detail, to examine the business models and to see how a company can grow without risking the balance sheet. These are two of my favorite companies in this space, but of course as with all stocks, whether they are good buys at any given time depends on the prevailing price as well as subsequent developments. And, as a quick glance at a long-term price graph of any of the stocks mentioned here will show, having a low-risk business model does not mean that the price of the stock is not volatile. But they are worth studying in a little more detail to gain insight into the model.

TAKING AN INNOVATIVE APPROACH TO BUILDING VALUE: A CASE STUDY

Altius has its roots as a prospect generator, focusing on mineral-rich but under-explored Newfoundland and Labrador. It has grown beyond that, but still looks at opportunities to grow using other people's money to advance projects and minimize risk. And it still generates properties; recently it staked three new uranium properties in central Newfoundland and a nickel property in the east with a plan to advance to a joint venture or strategic equity stake. Altius has seven main assets now, four of which are joint ventures or minority interests developed through staking. Let's look at these first.

*It holds 10% of Aurora Energy, a company exploring the Central Mineral Belt for uranium; engineering studies are underway on one property (Michelin). Recent exploration has confirmed potential for similar size on another property (Jacques Lake). Originally, Altius had vended out some uranium properties to Fronteer in a standard joint venture. Later, the companies spun out these assets in a separate public company (Aurora); Altius has sold down its interest (raising a total of CDN$104 million in 2006). It now holds 10% of the shares, valued in the market at CDN$97 million, plus owns a 2% gross sales royalty on the uranium (and a separate royalty on other metals) that may be produced on the property. This is a stunning example of Altius's business model, in using OPM (other people's money) to advance projects, while more than recouping its investment and retaining an interest in the project. Altius's original cost in this venture is CDN$661,000 only five years ago, so the return has been phenomenal.

*It owns 30% of London-listed Rambler Metals, which is planning on reopening the old Rambler gold-copper mine; recent strong results have expanded the resource. Altius's share is valued at a little over CDN$12 million. Again, Rambler developed originally out of a standard joint venture, but Altius is in a position to convert its equity into a royalty or sell down as the project develops.

*In addition, it is in other joint ventures, including a uranium property in western Newfoundland, joint-ventured with JNR Resources; and a new joint venture with Rubicon which spun off its diversified portfolio of early-stage Newfoundland properties which Altius partially funded, giving it 17% of Paragon Minerals.

*Altius also has two-dozen or more other properties, which it plans on joint venturing. Though not high priority, joint venturing these projects will generate work at little cost to Altius. Beyond the joint venture programs, Altius has three other very attractive ventures.

*It owns a royalty on Inco's Voisey's Bay nickel project which started operations just a year ago. This will generate about $1 million a quarter to Altius, with no cost, at today's nickel prices. This multi-decade project has plenty of exploration upside and great leverage to nickel prices.

*It is a partner and manager of the Newfoundland and Labrador Refining Corporation. A stroke of genius on the part of Altius: the NLRC, with investors from Ireland and the U.K. and in which Altius owns 37.5% as well as a royalty, is developing a proposal to build a new oil refinery in Placenta Bay in southeast Newfoundland.

A positive feasibility study shows robust returns after a capital cost of $4.6 billion. The proposed refinery would be strategically located close to the offshore East Canada oil fields as well as the oil-hungry North East United States, in one of the deepest ice-free ports in North America, in an area with high unemployment and a competitive workforce. An economic impact study is currently underway. If approved and the project proceeds, it would be a money spinner for Altius for decades into the future. In keeping with its business model, Altius would likely sell down its interest rather than raise the capital itself, perhaps keeping a smaller free-carried interest and royalty. Indeed, the next step could be for Altius to bring in a partner to fund its portion of the costs.

Equally importantly, perhaps, the successful development of the huge refinery project will showcase Altius as the partner of choice in the resource field in Newfoundland, and open the door to many other projects. Altius has also made a proposal to the provincial government for financing the Lower Churchill hydroelectric project. Its proposal was put on the three-bid short list; its proposal (involving a royalty foundation for provincial residents) has the benefit of providing jobs for the local populace, a sensitive issue in a poor province where many projects have been sold to outside interests. Altius's proposal could also be combined with other financing proposals. Currently, the provincial government is working on the development plan. Once this plan is complete, after three or four months perhaps, it will turn again to the financing proposals. If successful, Altius would would likely end up with a free-carried interest generating cash flow, for very little initial cost.

The company's main asset, however, without question is the president Brian Dalton, an unassuming but incredibly bright young man who developed the company by hard work, cost control, high ethics and intelligence. He has surrounded himself with bright people—often older, with great experience and stature.

Even though the price of Altius's stock has more than tripled since mid-2005, the whole company is valued at just under CDN$300 million. If one adds up the value of just the hard assets, one can see that Altius remains undervalued. Below are market values or conservative estimates of the main hard assets (as of February 2007):

- Aurora (equity share)   C$90 million
- Rambler (equity share)   C$12 million
- Voisey's Bay (royalty)   C$30 million

     Working capital   C$85 million

This gives a value of CDN$217 million without giving any value to the various joint ventures and exploration programs, (worth easily $25 million) nor to the high-potential refinery and hydro proposals. Even if neither of these were to pan out, therefore, Altius is not expensive, while the market appears to be giving no value at all to projects that could transform the company. This, despite the fact that the shares have done remarkably well in recent years, remains a company with low risk and high potential.

CASE STUDY #2: THE LEADING PROSPECT GENERATOR

Virginia Mines is a more traditional prospect generator, but has been very successful at it, recently selling its discovery of a major gold deposit at Eleonore to Goldcorp in return for shares and a royalty. This transaction was a good example of the way these companies often retain an interest in their projects while replenishing the balance sheet. It is also a good example of the patience that is required with prospect generators (and indeed exploration companies in general). Virginia stock did relatively little for many years until the Eleonore discovery and subsequent property acquisition by Goldcorp, which ultimately generated gains of over 2,000%. Now, once again Virginia is returning to its roots, generating prospects and joint venturing them.

Like many prospect generators, Virginia is inexpensive. It has cash and marketable securities (as of February 2007) of over $40 million (mostly cash). It also owns a royalty on which we can put a hard value. The royalty it negotiated with Goldcorp on the Eleonore property is very attractive. It is a net smelter royalty (not profits) on a sliding scale, beginning at 2% and moving up to 3.5% as the price of gold increases. Further, it is an advance royalty, meaning the Goldcorp must start paying even if the property is not brought into production within two years. This could represent up to $4 million dollars in the first year, with plenty of upside from both the gold price and from exploration potential. This has an NAV reasonably estimated at CDN$30 million.

Beyond that, it holds an extensive property portfolio in Quebec, including about 1,000 sq km of land in the Eleonore region, with almost half a million ounces of gold in resources at Post Lemoyne and La Grand Sud. In addition, there are about half a dozen active projects, in a range of minerals, throughout Quebec. These include the Corvet gold property, originally optioned to Placer Dome, but now because of the latter's acquisition, to Goldcorp. This property portfolio has received only modest attention in the last couple of years after the discovery of Eleonore, since all of the company's focus was on developing that property rapidly. Now that Goldcorp owns it, Virginia can return to developing its other highly-prospective properties. Virginia has about a dozen active projects in Quebec, with at least four and up to six drill programs this year. The current budget for exploration is CDN$16 million of which Virginia pays just over $3 million. The rest is paid by joint venture partners, and incentive tax grants. Now that's what I call leverage, and it beats the leverage obtained by putting all of one's balance sheet into drill holes on a single property.

In short, Virginia has a proven exploration team, lots of ground, multiple exploration and drilling targets, a great balance sheet, and a business model that allows them to leverage exploration while maintaining their balance sheet. The downside is low—the main "risk" is time, waiting for another discovery. So while spectacular returns can result from buying the right stock just before a wonderful discovery, a more proven method, and a considerably more consistent one, is to hold stocks of companies that employ a risk-minimization business model, and be patient, while good management teams work to build their companies over time.

Adrian Day is a recognized money manager with individual and institutional clients, with individualized accounts in both the global and resource areas. For information call 410-224-2037 or visit www.AdrianDayAssetManagement.com.

8

The Perfect Resource Exploration Stock

Dr. Russell McDougal

Does the perfect resource exploration company actually exist? Yes, it does. In fact there are lots of them in various sizes and stages. And the more you understand what it is that makes them so 'perfect', the higher your odds of success and the greater your profits will be in the resource sector.

There are three predominant stages of junior resource explorers:
1. Start-Ups
2. Exploration progress
3. Discovery

This chapter will discuss all three stages beginning with the "Start-Ups." The heavy lifting in global exploration is accomplished by the small, nimble and efficient Canadian companies labeled "Juniors." Without these companies the pipeline of global resource production would soon be empty. Our perfect explorer will, first of all, be headed up by the very best people . . . those with vision, a wealth of experience and a successful track record of achievement.

The overall mandate of management is to "find something" (of economic value, of course). Yet, this doesn't happen by accident. The ultimate success or failure hinges upon the way the company's strategies are formulated and implemented. The ideal start-up explorer will have a large land package and/or multiple properties under contract. They should be seeking world-class deposits in mining friendly and politically stable countries or jurisdictions. Employing grass roots exploration is another essential tactic of a start-up company. They will be staffed with or have access to geologists that are proficient at continually turning up promising early stage exploration properties. It is cheaper, by an order of magnitude, to find unexplored or under explored properties, than it is to do the riskier and more expensive drilling of the project.

Examples of early stage geological work done by the start-ups are soil, rock and stream sediment sampling or trenching. They also will do geochemical, geophysical, induced polarization, magnetic and other surveys. Researching and re-analyzing historical records can also prove beneficial. The most promising of these projects are then developed and showcased to larger and more financially endowed resource companies for further development. You will want to put the vast majority of your speculation funds into companies that espouse this *project generation* model. How about the capitalization and share structure of these start up companies?

A Toronto listing is the typical starting point. NASDAQ, AMEX and other global listings come later for those that are successful in their efforts. The company must be well funded, with several million dollars in the treasury. They also must have the ability to raise funds on an ongoing basis. You will want a tight share structure. For example, a company with a total of 30 million shares outstanding that is selling for at $0.50 per share would have a tiny market capitalization of $15 million. From this level, if they make a discovery, the share price and market cap should begin to multiply. It is imperative to fully understand the market caps of the companies you own or follow. For example, a company with a share price of $0.60 and 20 million shares issued ($12 million market cap) is in actuality "cheaper" than a company selling at $0.40 with 40 million shares out ($16 million market cap).

A market cap under $60 million is a reasonable range where most start-up exploration companies will be found. As company events progress, so too should the market cap. You also want frugal management that will not spend money or issue new shares unnecessarily. This will give the company the staying power it needs as it heads toward mega-success. Company management must also own a significant percent of the company (minimum 10%). If they don't believe in themselves enough to own a large portion of the company's stock, neither should you. Surprisingly, you can own a significant percentage of a start-up company should you so desire. For example, you could own 0.5% of stock X (selling at $0.10 with 60 million shares out) by purchasing 300,000 shares for $30,000. Two percent of this company would run you $120,000.

I am certainly not suggesting this unless it would represent a very small portion of your overall portfolio and only if you have done extreme due diligence on the company. In most cases, it is far better to spread your speculative funds among numerous companies. I bring this up just to give you a perspective as to how small these companies actually are. The risk/reward ratio is the highest in the start-up companies, and I always advise that you take your original investment off the table when a stock has doubled. At that point, the position then becomes "worry free."

Your odds for success will greatly increase as you learn the stages that junior resource explorers go through. And you will also want to form contacts and alliances to help you invest only in the most perfect juniors.

EXPLORATION PROGRESS

Now let's dive into the subsequent stages through which start-up companies evolve, from concept to implementation. Again, the companies that perform grass roots exploration provide the highest amount of leverage, but of course they also come with the greatest risk. But that risk can be reduced through diversification and prudent research. The perfect exploration stock will be adept at finding grass roots projects with vast potential. They may control as few as six such properties or as many as thirty.

The properties will ideally have a broad spectrum of target minerals . . . gold, silver, diamonds, zinc, lead, copper, uranium, molybdenum, etc. Oil and gas explorers should also have multiple irons in the fire by holding several properties. This provides more chances for success as well as a degree of diversification for you. Our perfect explorers will now perform early stage exploration on these properties. The goal is to find promising results so as to interest a larger company in footing the bill for the more expensive development of the property. The following quote is from AuEx Ventures, Inc., a Canadian junior that adheres closely to the joint venture model:

"AuEx Ventures, Inc. is a Nevada-focused precious metals exploration company with a current portfolio of 15 exploration projects in Nevada controlling over 40,000 acres of unpatented mining claims and fee land. Ten of the projects are in joint venture agreements with seven companies who provide exploration funding. The company applies the extensive Nevada exploration experience and high-end technical skills of its founders to search for and acquire new precious metal exploration projects that are then offered for joint venture."

You want as many quality joint ventures as you can get within your company portfolio. It's hardly surprising how many more discoveries are made when funds are being spent and drills are turning. What are the terms of these joint ventures? It's pretty much "Let's Make a Deal" as you will see a broad spectrum of arrangements made. Often the major company will buy in to the project by committing several million dollars in exploration funds over a two or three year time frame. This will entitle the major to a 60% or so interest in the ultimate value of the project. Our smaller grass roots explorer will often get a carried interest from that point forward. There may also be incentives for the major to earn an additional percentage of the deal by paying for feasibility studies, mine construction, etc.

With joint ventures in place our start-up company will start receiving more market attention. The share price and market cap should respond accordingly as the market understands the company's potential. Exploration progress may now take the company's market cap towards the $150 million range. As an early investor you may have purchased stock when the market cap was as low as $15 million to $30 million. That would be a five to tenfold return, and we're not yet at the discovery stage. Prudence would dictate that you take some profits off the table during such an opportune time frame. Some of these joint ventures will eventually lead to key discoveries and some will not. Either way, our project generator will continue to fill the pipeline with more projects and more joint ventures. The goal is to continue moving forward until there is an actual discovery. As the following quote from another Canadian junior, Cornerstone Capital Resources, Inc. suggests, frugality is a key factor:

"Of the $7.5 million in 2006 projected expenditures, fully 90% is provided by our joint venture partners, maintaining Corner-stone's Treasury position at a very healthy level. As of September 18th, 2006, our Treasury stood at $7.1 million and we expect to finish the year in a similar position."

Is it okay to stray from the joint venture model? A start-up company must have an extraordinary reason for going it alone. If initial exploration results are clearly of a world class nature it actually can be prudent to hold on to 100% of the deal. Virginia Gold did exactly this with their Canadian Eleonore gold property and ended up selling it outright to Goldcorp in a deal valued at $644 million to Virginia shareholders. Whether you invest in start-ups or in companies further along in the exploration process you will come to fully appreciate this project generation and joint venture model. So too, will your bank account.

DISCOVERY

Do you know that 'success' in junior resource investing can bring rewards that are unimaginable to most people? We've looked at the start-up procedures, concepts, philosophies and modes of implementation of our nimble and efficient Canadian juniors. And you have seen how the essential ingredient of 'great people' can add enormous value to a company. The ultimate success for a junior explorer is "discovery." And you may be astounded at the profit potential that can come your way when you own an exploration company that reaches this point. Let's first look at a particular Canadian junior—Esperanza Silver, and track exactly how their recent key mineral discovery in Peru came about. This company's story is particularly interesting and illuminating.

Esperanza was listed on the Toronto Stock Exchange (Venture section) in August of 2003 as a start-up company. Their mission was to focus on early-stage silver and mineral exploration and development projects. The company targeted opportunities in Mexico, Bolivia and Peru. Esperanza came to my attention in late 2004, primarily because of the people involved in structuring the company. One of their directors was, at that time, Robert Quartermain of Silver Standard Resources (SSRI). Mr. Quartermain is simply the brightest and the best when it comes to building a silver company. John Prochnau and Paul Bartos were also directors with stellar reputations. William Pincus, an experienced geologist, was Esperanza's CEO after being in the industry some 25 years. This is exactly what you look for in resource exploration—highly experienced operators. The share structure was also quite appealing around that time as there were less than 25 million shares outstanding and the stock could be purchased in the $0.40 to $0.50 range (Canadian). At a market cap of $13 million, this company was definitely in the 'nano-cap' category. Esperanza subsequently entered into a joint venture agreement with Silver Standard "to prospect for new bulk mineable silver deposits in central Peru." How they carried out this venture is quite the story.

Looking for land areas of particular interest, these savvy geologists first combed through historical archives dating back to the 1950s. Old data can be worth a fortune and is frequently purchased to be reviewed with new eyes and more modern technology. Having found a particular area of interest they set about to explore it further. They drove as close as they could to this isolated area and then set up camp. They loaded their picks and supplies on donkeys and with a local farmer as a guide, they hiked to the area of interest near a lake. They were not disappointed as they found a number of quartz outcrops that held a particular appeal with the silver-seeking geologists. The farmer noticed that they liked the rocks. So he told them something to the effect of, "If you like these rocks, I know a canyon nearby that has a lot of them." So they took a detour on the way back to camp. The geologists liked the look of these rocks as well and took more samples.

Back home, when the rocks were finally assayed, they showed a promising amount of gold within them, especially in the area the farmer pointed out. Esperanza then went about staking claims with the Peruvian government covering these areas. Since that time Esperanza has done a lot of surface work on the property and found five large and rich gold/silver veins. It all looked extremely promising but it was totally unknown exactly how *deep* the veins extended. That question was partially answered in the last couple weeks as the results of four drill holes into the Ayelen vein showed that high-grade mineralization extends at least 50 meters deep on this particular vein.

Yes, it's perfectly okay to find gold even though you set out to find silver. It's called serendipity. But in this case, it is also called geological excellence. What they have found to date is gold/silver mineralization in grades up to two ounces of 'gold equivalent' per ton. These are eye-popping numbers and this is now a confirmed "discovery." Still, this is early stage drilling with only four holes completed. Total depths have to be drilled.

The other veins have to be drilled. The ground between the veins requires exploration. The entire area needs modern exploration, as there is the distinct possibility that a new gold/silver district has been found.

Esperanza has recently traded as high as $3.90 Canadian and now has a market cap well north of $100 million. They do not own 100% of this discovery because they were in a joint venture with Silver Standard in this deal. They could end up with a carried interest of 20% in the end, if and when a mine is established. But even this 20% should prove to be a grand slam home run. It's now up to the drills (truth machines) to determine exactly how large this project will grow. I am not making a recommendation of this stock; rather I am just using it to illustrate how a junior resource company goes from start up to discovery. Going from a market cap in the low teens to one well above $100 million is a fantastic achievement for any start-up company. What will likely happen in the end to Esperanza and their shareholders? They should eventually be richly rewarded by cash or shares in another company as they become an acquisition target. What they won't do is mine this project themselves! The gains will be taken and the company and/or personnel will likely move on in one form or another to the next grassroots project.

Here are some other examples of tiny explorers reaching the pinnacle:

1. Argentina Gold was bought by Homestake Gold in a deal valued at $270 million.
2. Francisco Gold was bought by Glamis Gold in a deal valued at $284 million.
3. Virginia Gold was bought by Goldcorp in a deal valued at $444 million Canadian.
4. Sutton Resources was bought by Barrick Gold in a deal valued at $493 million.
5. Arequipa was bought by Barrick Gold in a deal valued at $940 million.

6. Diamond Fields was bought by Inco in a deal valued around $2 billion.

While these examples demonstrate extreme success in the industry, only the very best out of the thousands of global explorers reach these heights. Fortunately, there are many ways to profit from the most elite explorers short of these ideals. The task at hand is to tap into the next nano-cap companies that will present a risk/reward ratio that is difficult for a seasoned speculator to pass up.

9

"How Much Is That"

A Primer for Converting Terms and Numbers Used to Describe Mineral Deposits Into Dollar Value and Stock Price

Brian Fagan

Mastering the art of correctly evaluating the dollar value of mineral exploration stocks can make you more money in the market than you ever dreamed of! Investors soon learn the six fundamental considerations used to identify companies that merit further consideration. The first five are easy. Look for good management, the ability to finance, a reasonable market capitalization, real asset value, and a comparatively low stock price. The sixth fundamental, the project, is where the confusion begins. Few outside of the industry can translate the terms and numbers used to describe mineral projects into a dollar value and equivalent stock price. Every investor, however, can do it by separating the task into three manageable parts. Combined, they result in a ballpark estimate of what the stock can be expected to trade at.

PART 1: DISTANCE & AREA

The first series of numbers encountered usually have to do with distance and area. Where is the property located? How big is it? What are its dimensions? What size are the mineralized structures? If the numbers used do not create a familiar picture of size in your mind, you are already lost as far as answering these simple yet important questions. The problem arises because companies still use both the Metric and Avoirdupois (inch/pound) systems of weights and measures to describe themselves. This condition will continue until the United States of America eventually changes to metric. When that might happen, who knows? Today, few Americans can mentally picture a property located 187 kilometers from some reference point, consisting of 640 hectares, where mineralized veins ranging from 2 to 80 centimeters are encountered in a zone measuring 250 x 1,300 meters.

To solve this problem, part one dissects and explains the relationship of the numbers you typically encounter evaluating these companies. All that is needed are a few easily remembered rules of thumb. Use them and the accompanying conversion tables to translate the unfamiliar into the system you can visualize. One day you will find that either system of numbers brings up the same mental picture of distance or size. Then the mystery of "how far or how big is that?" will be gone forever.

Now that automobile speedometers show both kilometers (km.) and miles (mi.), most North Americans have a sense of how fast they are going in either system. How far they are going is a different question. The magic number to remember is 100 km. = 62 mi. Runners have no problem with this; they know a 10K run is 6.2 miles. For short distances, using 5 km. = 3 mi. will keep you in the ballpark. It is important to be able to visualize how far a property is from other significant deposits, and even more so to have a clear picture of the length and width of the regional mineralized structures.

The metric unit used to describe specific zones of mineralization is the meter (m.), the close equivalent of a U.S. yard (yd.). There are 1,000 m. in 1 km.; that equates to 3,280.8 ft., roughly the length of 9 U.S. football fields. Trenches, drill plans, the length of drill holes, and their mineralized sections are reported in m. To visualize m., the non-metric person sees them in feet (ft.). Rule of thumb: 1 m. = 3 ft., 3 m. = 10 ft., 10 m. = 33 ft.

The smallest metric unit you are likely to encounter is the centimeter (cm.). There are 2.54 cm. in 1 inch (in.). Canadian ski conditions are reported in centimeters. When the resort you're heading to is reporting a base of 107 cm., you can expect to find 3.5 feet of snow on the slopes. In mining, the use of cm. never exceeds 100 cm., the equivalent of 1m. This makes it simple to visualize. Look at any ruler with both scales and you will find 30.5 cm. in 1 ft. That's all you have to remember to see these little guys clearly.

Granted, many U.S. investors are comfortable working with distance in metric, but how many can visualize the size of a property described in square kilometers (sq. km.) or worse yet in hectares (ha.). The U.S. equivalents would be square miles (sq. mi.) and acres (ac.), which we can all see. Even after working in the field for years, I cannot visualize the size of an area in hectares without first converting them to sq. km., or ac. and then sq. mi. Let's try to picture a hectare.

One ha. contains 10,000 sq. m., and one sq. ha. measures 100x100 m. That is slightly less than the area of two U.S. football fields. One hundred ha. equals 1 sq. km., and a sq. km. measures 1,000 X 1,000 m. A person brought up in metric will clearly visualize these sizes and relate to the football fields in meters. To go the other way, 1 ha. = 2.471 ac., and 640 ac. = 1 sq. mi. The rule of thumb for these conversions is 260 ha. = 1 sq. mi. To keep things simple, use the tables on page 86.

Today, there are a few companies reporting mineral interests in excess of one million hectares. How big is that? It is very, very big—exactly 3,861 sq. mi. If the property were 20 mi. wide it would be 193 mi. long. In a light aircraft it would take more than an hour to fly over; on the ground, it is going to take years and a lot of cash to explore. So as long as the company has the money, you can count on exposure for many field seasons. The reverse also holds true. A property consisting of 1,000 ha. is slightly less than 4 sq. mi. If nothing of interest is found in one or two field seasons of diligent exploration, it's probably game over.

PART 2: SIZE AND GRADE

Determining the right price to buy or sell a stock requires you to estimate the value of its underlying assets. For mineral exploration companies the valuation starts with a calculation of *size* and *grade* for each of its mineral deposits. Companies try their best to give investors all the information needed to make this calculation, but it's always in unfamiliar terminology. Part 1 takes the mystery out of converting the two scales used to calculate *size.* The next step is to be able to convert the reported *grade* into a dollar value equivalent.

BASE METALS

The end objective in calculating grade is to convert the metal content, in the weight unit of rock that is being mined and reported, into a dollar amount. This dollar amount is calculated in the weight unit the metal is quoted and sold in. Base metals are quoted and sold in the Avoirdupois pound unit. Avoirdupois is the system of weights (used in the United States) for common commodities such as base metals, coal, grain, and foodstuffs. Base metal grade is calculated in metric, and then reported as a percent of the avoirdupois ton (2,000 pounds) or metric tonne (2,204.622 pounds).

A mineral deposit in the United States would be described in the avoirdupois system. If it contains 200 million tons of rock grading one percent copper, it would contain 20 lb. copper in each ton of rock, or 4 billion contained pounds copper total **(2,000 lb. in one avoirdupois ton X 0.01 grade = 20 lb. copper/ton X 200,000,000 tons = 4 billion lb. copper total).** With copper selling at $3.00 per lb., each ton of rock has a contained gross metal value of $60. The total deposit has a gross metal value of $12 billion.

The numbers for a similar deposit located in a metric country would be different. It would be described as containing 200 million tonnes (metric tonnes) grading one percent copper. Each tonne of rock would contain 22.05 lb. copper, or 4.41 billion contained pounds copper total (**2,204.622 lb. in one metric tonne X 0.01 grade = 22.05 lb. copper/tonne X 200,000,000 tonnes = 4.41 billion lb. copper total**). At $3 per pound copper, each tonne of rock has a contained gross metal value of $66.15; the total deposit is $13.23 billion. There is no mystery in this; all the numbers increase by the 10% pound difference between the avoirdupois ton and the metric tonne.

This simple math gives you the two basic numbers from which a value judgment on grade and size begins. 1) When the contained gross dollar metal value in each ton or tonne of rock is known, engineers and savvy investors immediately have a good idea if the rock can be mined and the metal extracted profitably. The ballpark cost of mining and processing is estimated; if it is less than the host rock's contained gross metal value, a mine may be possible. When you hear someone say, "that's $60 rock," they are talking about the gross contained dollar metal value of the size unit (ton or tonne) to be mined. 2) Knowing the contained gross metal value for the total deposit enables you to assess its economic importance and the effect it might ultimately have on the company's stock price. Most of the base metals are reported and can be calculated in this manner. Precious metals are a different story and a bit more complicated.

PRECIOUS METALS

The confusion in calculating *size* stems from the practice of reporting it in both the metric and inch/pound measurement systems; for the *grade* of base metals it's metric and avoirdupois. This situation prevails and gets even more confusing with the addition of a third system for reporting the weights of precious metals. **TROY WEIGHT is the system of weights used for precious metals and gems. The equivalents are: 24 grains = 1 penny weight; 20 penny-weights = 1 ounce; 12 ounces = 1 pound. The troy grain is the same as the avoirdupois grain, but the ounce is larger on the troy scale; 1 ounce troy = 31.1035 grams; 1 ounce avoirdupois = 28.35 grams.** This gets worse as we encounter grade reported in *grams gold per metric tonne*; this is the standard outside of the United States. World gold statistics are reported in metric tonnes. Is there a common denominator? Yes! Estimate the deposit's value in the dollar value of the contained precious metals—in the weight unit (ton or tonne) the mine is or will be processing.

The world quotes, buys, and sells its gold in troy ounces; that's the only ounce gold ever comes in. Precious metal grades, however, are reported in troy ounces per avoirdupois ton and troy ounces per metric tonne or grams per metric tonne, or sometimes even grams per avoirdupois ton. Once again, the objective is to convert the different types of reporting into a dollar amount you can use to establish value.

Companies reporting gold grades in ounces per ton or tonne pose no problem. Multiply the gold price by the grade, (**$600 X 0.25 grade oz./ton or oz./tonne gold and we are talking $150 rock**). Each ton or tonne of rock contains $150 worth of gold. For mines reporting grade in grams, there are two simple conversion figures used to convert grams to ounces. I'm going to take you through the math so you will know where these numbers are derived from.

GRAMS GOLD PER METRIC TONNE
TROY OUNCES GOLD PER METRIC TONNE

GRAMS GOLD PER AVOIRDUPOIS TON
TROY OUNCES GOLD PER AVOIRDUPOIS TON

Even though one metric tonne contains 1,000,000 grams and an avoirdupois ton contains 907,185 grams, the math for both these conversions is exactly the same. I have illustrated it in metric tonnes. If you find yourself working in tons, substitute ton for tonne in the example and it will work. The math here is really simple. Divide the reported grams per metric tonne by 31.1035, the weight of one troy ounce, to get ounces per metric tonne. (**15.555175 g./mt. ÷ 31.1035 = 0.50 oz./mt.**). Now that you know it works, keep it simple by using 31.1. **A deposit averaging 3.11 g./mt. gold is going to contain on average 0.10 oz. gold in each mt. of rock (3.11 g./mt. ÷ 31.1 grams per troy ounce = 0.10 oz. gold/mt.).**

With gold selling at $600/ounce ($600 X 0.10 = $60), we are talking $60 rock. When gold is reported in this manner for deposits measured and mined in metric, it keeps things simple. You know how many grams or ounces of gold there are in each metric tonne. If you know the number of metric tonnes in the deposit you know the total gold content. Factor in the gold price and you know its dollar value.

GRAMS GOLD PER METRIC TONNE
TO
TROY OUNCES GOLD PER AVOIRDUPOIS TON

This is the tough one! It remains a mystery to me why companies reporting in metric often report gold in grams per metric tonne and then in ounces per avoirdupois ton. They mine and publish their reserves in metric tonnes, but then, with this type of reporting, require you to convert the tonnes to tons before you can know how much gold they have. Adding further confusion, you then have to convert the grams per metric tonne to ounces per metric tonne to **know what $ amount rock they are talking.** Still, reporting in this manner is common and should be understood.

One metric tonne (mt.) = 2,204.622 pounds (lb.), and 1 troy ounce (oz.) = 31.1035 grams (g.). If 1 mt. contains 1 oz. of gold, it contains 31.1035 g. gold in 2,204.622 lb. of rock. Each lb. of rock contains 0.014108 g. of gold. (31.1035 g. in 1 ounce of gold ÷ 2,204.622 lb. in one metric tonne = 0.014108 g. gold in 1 lb.).

If there were only 2,000 lb. of this rock (1 avoirdupois ton), it would contain 28.216 g. gold (2,000 lb. rock X 0.014108 g. gold per lb. = 28.216 g. gold per ton). The difference is simply the 10% weight difference between the avoirdupois ton and metric tonne (204.622 ÷ 2,000 = 0.1023). The factor for converting gram/metric tonne to ounce/ton must also change by this ten percent (31.1035 g./oz. X 0.1023 weight factor = 3.1819 g.). Add this 3.1819 g. difference to the standard 31.1035 g./oz. and you get 34.2854, which is the conversion factor for going from grams per metric tonne to troy ounces per avoirdupois ton. Simple? No, but it can be simplified.

You can now round off the 34.2854 to a conversion factor of **34.3.** Dividing the reported grams per metric tonne by 34.3 = ounces per avoirdupois ton. Note the same ten percent difference inherent throughout this conversion **(31.1 g./mt. gold grade ÷ 34.3 conversion factor = 0.90 oz./ton gold).**

GRAMS PER METRIC TONNE	GRAMS PER AVOIRDUPOIS TON			OUNCES PER AVOIRDUPOIS TON	OUNCES PER METRIC TONNE
G	G	1	0.0322	O	O
R	R	2	0.0643	U	U
A	A	3	0.0965	N	N
M	M	4	0.1286	C	C
S	S	5	0.1608	E	E
		6	0.1929	S	S
P	P	7	0.2251		
E	E	8	0.2572	P	P
R	R	9	0.2894	E	E
		10	0.3215	R	R
M	A	11	0.3537		
E	V	12	0.3858	A	M
T	O	13	0.4180	V	E
R	I	14	0.4501	O	T
I	R	15	0.4823	I	R
C	D	16	0.5144	R	I
	U	17	0.5466	D	C
T	P	18	0.5787	U	
O	O	19	0.6109	P	T
N	I	20	0.6430	O	O
N	S	21	0.6752	I	N
E		22	0.7073	S	N
	T	23	0.7395		E
	O	24	0.7716	T	
	N	25	0.8038	O	
		26	0.8359	N	
		27	0.8681		
		28	0.9002		
		29	0.9324		
		30	0.9645		

GRAMS PER METRIC TONNE			OUNCES PER AVOIRDUPOIS TON
G	1	0.0292	O
R	2	0.0583	U
A	3	0.0875	N
M	4	0.1167	C
S	5	0.1458	E
	6	0.1750	S
P	7	0.2042	
E	8	0.2333	P
R	9	0.2625	E
	10	0.2917	R
M	11	0.3208	
E	12	0.3500	A
T	13	0.3792	V
R	14	0.4083	O
I	15	0.4375	I
C	16	0.4667	R
	17	0.4958	D
T	18	0.5250	U
O	19	0.5542	P
N	20	0.5833	O
N	21	0.6125	I
E	22	0.6417	S
	23	0.6708	
	24	0.7000	T
	25	0.7292	O
	26	0.7583	N
	27	0.7875	
	28	0.8167	
	29	0.8458	
	30	0.8750	

HOW IT WORKS

The grades for gold deposits located in the United States are reported in oz./ton gold. Let's say the deposit is 50 million tons grading 0.08 oz./ton gold, and gold is selling at $600 per ounce. The deposit would contain 4 million ounces and have a contained gross metal dollar value of $2.4 billion **(1 ton X 0.08 oz./ton gold grade = 0.08 oz./ton X $600 = $48 per ton X 50 million tons = $2.4 billion ÷ $600 = 4 million ounces).** Each ton of rock would have a contained gross metal value of $48. **We're talking $48 rock here.** Try this exercise on a few company news releases and you'll get a whole new perspective on the significance of the numbers.

A deposit containing the same 4 million ounces at the same grade would be reported in metric as 50 million tonnes with a grade of 2.48824 g./tonne gold. Here's the math: **31.1035 g./oz. X 0.08 oz./tonne gold grade = 2.48824 g./tonne gold grade X 50 million tonnes = 124,412,000 total contained grams gold ÷ 31.1035 g./oz. = 4 million contained ounces gold.** It's the same. The deposit's total contained gross metal value and the dollar value per tonne are also the same. The difference is that the 4 million ounces of gold are contained in 10% more rock, the same 10% tonne to ton lb. ratio.

PPM & PPB TO OUNCES
PER TON OR TONNE

The only other way gold grade is reported is in PPM and PPB. They are functions of the metric tonne and convert instantly into grams. PPM stands for Parts Per Million. The metric tonne contains 1 million grams. Therefore, in reporting the grade for any precious metal 1 PPM = 1 gram. PPB stands for Parts Per Billion. The equivalents are: 1,000 PPB = 1 PPM = 1 gram. PPB is used only when the gold content is very, very low—less than one gram. Beware of large numbers in PPB; they need to be divided by 1,000 to equal grams. When you see PPM or PPB, convert their gram equivalents into ounces per ton or tonne, then to the dollar amount you need to estimate value.

TIME TO RELAX

After all this, all you need to remember are two conversion factors: **31.1** and **34.3**. Even if you make a mistake with these factors the error will not exceed 10%, well within the limits for assigning a value to a developing gold stock. I, too, must admit to being a little overwhelmed with all these conversions of *size* and *grade*. Now when they are used to estimate the value of a deposit and the price of a stock, our patience will be rewarded.

DISTANCE EQUIVALENTS						
KM.	METER	CM.	MILE	YARD	FEET	INCH
1 km.	1,000 m.		0.6214 mi.	1,093.6 yd.	3,280.8 ft.	
	1 m.	100 cm.		1,093.6 yd.	3.2808 ft.	39.37079 in.
		1 cm.				0.3937 in.
1.6093 km.	1,609.3 m.		1 mi.	1,760 yd.	5,280 ft.	
	1,609.3 m.	91.44 cm.		1 yd.	3 ft.	36 in.
	1,609.3 m.	30.48 cm.			1 ft.	12 in.
		2.54 cm.				1 in.

AREA EQUIVALENTS

SQ. KM.	HECTARE	SQ. METER	SQ. MILE	ACRE	SQ. YARD	SQ. FEET
1 sq. km.	100 ha.	1,000,000 sq. m.	0.386 sq. mi.	247.1 ac.	1,196,000. sq. yd.	
0.01 sq. km.	**1 ha.**	10,000 sq. m.	0.0038 sq. mi.	2.471 ac.	11,960 sq. yd.	
		1 sq. m.			1.196 sq. yd.	10.764 sq. ft.
2.590 sq. km.	259 ha.		**1 sq. mi.**	640 ac.		
	0.4047 ha.	4,047 sq. m.		**1 ac.**	4,840. sq. yd.	43,560 sq. ft.
		0.836 sq. m.			**1 sq. yd.**	9 sq. ft.
		0.093 sq. m.				**1 sq. ft.**

AREA EQUIVALENTS

HECTARES	SQ. KM.	SQ. MI.	ACRES
100	1	0.386	247.1
200	2	0.772	494.2
300	3	1.158	741.3
400	4	1.544	988.4
500	5	1.93	1,235.50
1,000	10	3.86	2,471.00
2,000	20	7.72	4,942.00
3,000	30	11.58	7,413.00
4,000	40	15.44	9,884.00
5,000	50	19.3	12,355.00
6,000	60	23.16	14,826.00
7,000	70	27.02	17,297.00
8,000	80	30.88	19,768.00
9,000	90	34.74	22,239.00
10,000	100	38.6	24,710.00
20,000	200	77.2	49,420.00
30,000	300	115.8	74,130.00
40,000	400	154.4	98,840.00
50,000	500	193	123,550.00
60,000	600	231.6	148,260.00
70,000	700	270.2	172,970.00
80,000	800	308.8	197,680.00
90,000	900	347.4	222,390.00
100,000	1,000	386	247,100.00
200,000	2,000	772	494,200.00
300,000	3,000	1,158.00	741,300.00
400,000	4,000	1,544.00	988,400.00
500,000	5,000	1,930.00	1,235,500.00
600,000	6,000	2,316.00	1,482,600.00
700,000	7,000	2,702.00	1,729,700.00
800,000	8,000	3,088.00	1,976,800.00
900,000	9,000	3,474.00	2,223,900.00
1,000,000	10,000	3,860.00	2,471,000.00
HECTARES	SQ. KM.	SQ. MI.	ACRES

AREA EQUIVALENTS

ACRES	SQ. MI.	SQ. KM.	HECTARES
100	0.1563	0.4047	40.47
200	0.3126	0.8094	80.94
300	0.4685	1.2141	121.41
400	0.6252	1.6188	161.88
500	0.7815	2.0235	202.35
1,000	1.563	4.047	404.7
2,000	3.126	8.094	809.4
3,000	4.689	12.141	1,214.10
4,000	6.252	16.188	1,618.80
5,000	7.815	20.235	2,023.50
6,000	9.378	24.282	2,428.20
7,000	10.941	28.329	2,832.90
8,000	12.504	32.376	3,237.60
9,000	14.067	36.423	3,642.30
10,000	15.63	40.47	4,047.00
20,000	31.26	80.94	8,094.00
30,000	46.89	121.41	12,141.00
40,000	62.52	161.88	16,188.00
50,000	78.15	202.35	20,235.00
60,000	93.78	242.82	24,282.00
70,000	109.41	283.29	28,329.00
80,000	125.04	323.76	32,376.00
90,000	140.67	364.23	36,423.00
100,000	156.3	404.7	40,470.00
200,000	312.6	809.4	80,940.00
300,000	468.9	1,214.10	121,410.00
400,000	625.2	1,618.80	161,880.00
500,000	781.5	2,023.50	202,350.00
600,000	937.8	2,428.20	242,820.00
700,000	1,094.10	2,832.90	283,290.00
800,000	1,250.40	3,237.60	323,760.00
900,000	1,406.70	3,642.30	364,230.00
1,000,000	1,563.00	4,047.00	404,700.00
ACRES	SQ. MI.	SQ. KM.	HECTARES

PART 3: CONVERTING SIZE & GRADE TO STOCK PRICE

Starting with the total area of a property, you can work your way down through the many decreasing units of size used to describe the potential of a particular project. The end result is to estimate the property's present value and open ended potential. A company that has identified a zone of mineralization and owns a large track of ground around it is the most favorable situation. Once a discovery has been made, the odds for finding additional mineralization in the nearby area are greatly enhanced. Companies with small land positions that host defined zones of mineralization are often preferable to those with larger but unexplored properties.

AIRBORNE ANOMALIES

Company news releases usually start with the size of the property, then state that within its boundaries certain areas with elevated potential for discovery have been identified. These areas will be referred to as zones delineated by some type of *anomaly.* The word *anomaly* is defined as: something irregular or abnormal, any deviation from uniformity. As a geological term it is used to denote and describe a distinctive local feature on the ground. There are many types of anomalies.

In areas of difficult access, initial prospecting is often done from the air. Geologists in light aircraft and helicopters look for *color anomalies.* These are areas where the surface has turned red, white, green, or yellow from the weathering of sulfide minerals associated with ore deposits. Simple as it may sound, this is an effective method. The magnificent Voisey's Bay deposit of Diamond Fields (then INCO—now CVRD Inco Ltd.) started off with the recognition of a color anomaly. An area of concentrated local mining activity or old workings is another anomalous signature looked for. Sophisticated airborne anomalies are obtained from aerial photography, airborne geophysical surveys, satellite landsat images, and radarsat. Everything looks good from the air! Further ground follow-up investigation is needed, and that is where our measurements begin.

GRIDS AND GRID LINES

There is no sense in collecting any substantial amount of data from the surface unless you can find your way back to the exact location it was gathered from and tie it in with all other data locations. Some sort of ground control is necessary. This is accomplished by establishing a series of grid lines over the area to be explored. You see this in almost every news release when surface work begins in a new area. "The company has established (so many kilometers/miles) of grid line on the property and will now start to conduct its various survey programs." Since just about all the measurements you are interested in originate from some sort of grid, it is useful to know what one looks like. (Grids and grid lines all resemble the one pictured below on page 94.)

They are physically put in place and marked off on the ground at predetermined intervals. If the area is covered with vegetation, it is cut and removed along the lines. This is where the term "cutting grid lines" comes from. Since metric is the standard in use today, it is used throughout this chapter. The first line to go in is called the base line. Its direction is determined by the inferred strike (long axis) of the mineralized zone. For convenience I'm using south to north. A 100 meter grid with 100 meter markings is an often used initial grid size. The first physical marker, usually a wooden picket, put in to start the base line is marked 00+00. As it goes north 100 meters, the next picket is put in and marked 00+100N. One hundred meters further north the next picket reads 00+200N. The base line can go on indefinitely and often does for many kilometers. Grid lines run perpendicular east and west to the base line at each 100 meter interval. Look at the intersecting line at 00+500N on the base line to see how it is marked. The first picket 100 meters east of the base line is marked 500N+100E. The next one, another 100 meters east, reads 500N+200E. Going west from the base line they read 500N+100W, then 500N+200W, and on and on. Standing at a picket marked 3000N+700W (not shown), you are 3 kilometers north and 700 meters west of the 00+00 picket, the beginning of the base line. Any number of closer spaced grids can be established within the main one. In this simple manner everyone knows where they are and where every bit of data gathered from the property came from. With the grid in place the surface surveys can begin.

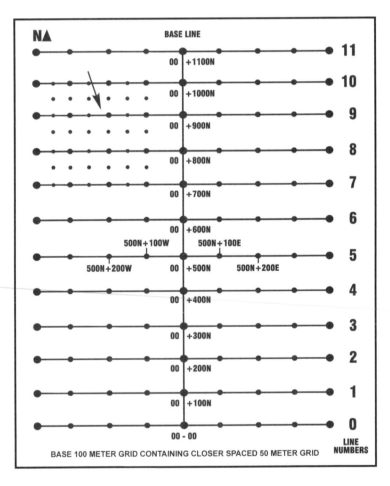

BASE 100 METER GRID CONTAINING CLOSER SPACED 50 METER GRID

SURFACE SURVEYS AND ANOMALIES

There are three basic surface surveys used in early stage exploration: geological, geophysical, and geochemical. They all provide different data that are interpreted collectively to determine the location of areas to trench and where to spot drill holes. There is no mystery to a geological survey. It consists of walking the ground, initially along the cleared grid lines, and making a map of surface geologic characteristics. These include the various rock types, their alteration signatures, and structural features. Many times mineralization favors a particular type of rock and is associated with a structural zone of weakness in the earth's crust.

The events that deposit minerals often alter the surrounding rocks in some way during the process. An example of a rock type anomaly could be a rock unit containing many small quartz veins. In many alteration anomalies the original hard rock has been altered to clay. Structural anomalies may be fault or shear zones where rock units have moved in relation to each other and shattered, allowing mineralizing solutions to penetrate the zone. Because their locations are tied into the grid, their measurements are easily determined. This information will be the first hint as to what the size potential of the property may be.

Geophysical surveys are conducted over areas identified by geological or previous airborne geophysical ones. These anomalies come in a variety of forms, such as gravity, magnetic, induced polarization, and many more. Basically, they are a measurement of the magnetism, electrical conductivity, or resistivity of the ground. When it varies from the surrounding area, you have a geophysical anomaly that may or may not be related to a mineral deposit. The interpretation of geophysics is reserved for the experts in that field. Suffice it to say, the bigger the size and the greater the variance from its surroundings, the better. The locations of the readings taken to produce them are also tied to the grid. When the results are plotted and contoured on it, the size, strength, and location of the anomaly is known.

When near-surface gold is the target, geochemical surveys provide the best indicative data. They consist of taking soil or rock chip samples at specific locations on or tied into the grid lines, then analyzing them for their mineral content. Like the geophysical readings, these results are plotted and contoured on the grid. Immediately, you can tell where the sought after mineral is present and in what amount. If it doesn't show up at all I tend to lose interest in the project, even if other trace elements that usually occur with it are present. If gold is being looked for, I want to see gold in the geochemical surface survey. Gold geochemistry and the occurrence of gold in soils is far from being an exact science; however, gold in rock chips from outcrop is the next best thing to the results obtained from trenching. The saying goes "gold is where you find it." Whenever you see interesting gold assays or anomalies, the company deserves further investigation.

When one type of anomaly occupies the same location as another, they are said to be coincident. If all the anomalies stack up as they do in the diagram on page 97, the results of the surface surveys are screaming that it's time to drill. In quiet markets all the above information will be available before the stock has had a big move. Paying attention to this type of data, and interpreting it correctly, can get you in on a very good story early.

SIZE & SIGNIFICANCE OF ANOMALIES

Unless the anomaly is so large that it is in fact a regional feature (incorrectly reported as an anomaly), the bigger it is the better. That is the point companies try to impart when reporting them. To get a handle on their size and significance, first convert their measurements into surface area by multiplying length X width = square meters. Then convert the area figure to cubic meters by multiplying it by a reasonably expected vertical depth for the deposit. Finally, convert the cubic meters to a metric tonne equivalent. The math is simple. Length X width X depth X conversion factor = metric tonnes. Recently, I was looking at a deposit that had a drill indicated vertical depth of at least 350 meters. That is exceptional! So let's just use 200 meters of vertical depth in this example with a gold anomaly measuring 1,000 meters in length by 300 meters in width on surface.

How would a promoter present the picture? Naturally, he projects the yet to be drilled deposit to be as big as the anomaly. **1,000m length X 300m width X 200m depth = 60 million cubic meters.**

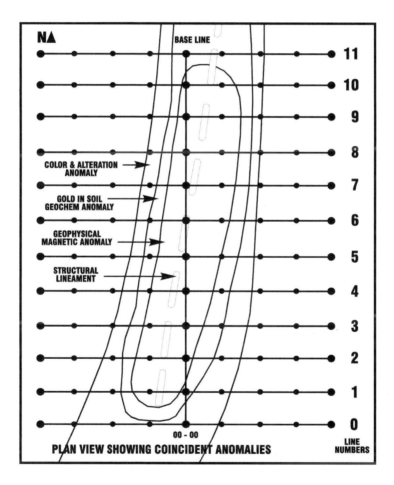

To convert cubic meters to tonnes you need to know how many tonnes there are in one cubic meter. That depends on the character of the ore (get this number from the company). This number is very important and can vary more than 100%. A massive sulfide nickel ore may have a specific gravity over 4 (four). For our example of an oxidized disseminated gold deposit it's about 2.6 tonnes per cubic meter. **60 million cubic meters X 2.6 = 156 million tonnes.** The promoter figures it will grade 1.5 grams per tonne and the gold will have a value of US$50 per ounce in the ground. The company will have 10 million shares issued on a fully diluted basis. To keep the numbers small, start by converting the grade from grams to ounces. **1.5 grams /tonne ÷ 31.1035 grams/troy ounce = 0.0482 ounce/tonne.** The total amount of gold in the deposit would then be 156 million X 0.0482 ounce gold/tonne = 7.5 million ounces. Valuing the gold at US$50 per ounce the company would be worth: **US$50 X 7.5 million ounces = US$375 million X 1.10 US/CDN rate = CDN$412.5 million ÷ 10 million shares issued = CDN$41.25 per share. Read on before you call your broker.**

Let's inject some reality into the promoter's dreams. Only about one out of every one thousand anomalies drilled becomes a mine. Even when this appears likely to happen, the above numbers should be substantially discounted. Gold deposits are never as wide as their signature anomalies, so let's reduce the width of this one by 2/3 to 100 meters and the price for gold in the ground by 1/2 to US$25 per ounce. The rest is plausible. The math works out to this: **1,000 m.l. X 100 m.w. X 200 m.d. X 2.6 = 52 million tonnes X 0.0482 oz. gold/t. = 2.5 million ounces gold X US$25 = US$62.5 million X 1.10 = CDN$68.75 million ÷ 10 million shares = CDN$6.88 per share.** As you can see, these numbers are all over the map, but a few drill holes return-ing long intersections grading 1.5 grams gold/tonne could take this stock to the $6–$10 level. If it is trading around $2 before the drilling begins and you like the target, you should buy the stock.

TRENCHING & TRENCH RESULTS

Trenching is the next program normally undertaken to further understand and delineate a deposit. When the overburden above a deposit is shallow enough so that the depth of the trench reaches actual hard rock in place, trench results give a very good indication of what you can expect to get in the drilling. The plan-view on page 100 shows the location and assay results of five trenches excavated on the grid. The mineralized sections of these trenches average out to be 75 meters in width, grading 3 grams gold per tonne. Trench 1, since it returned no values, would indicate the southern extent of the zone. There are no trenches north of trench 5, indicating the zone may continue further north. The strike length between trench 2 and trench 5 is 1,000 meters. The mathematics for converting size and grade results from anomalies, trenches, and drilling always remains the same.

In this case it would be: **1,000m length X 75m width X 200m projected depth X 2.6 conversion factor = 39 million tonnes X 0.0965 oz/t grade (3g/t ÷ 31.1035 g/troy oz) = 3.76 million contained ounces gold X US$25 value of one ounce in the ground = US$94 million value X 1.10 US/CDN exchange rate = CDN$103.4 million value ÷ 10 million shares issued = CDN$10.34 per share.** Speculating on drill holes that will test the down dip extension of good trench results is about as good as it gets in early stage drill programs. Because these stocks will already have had an increase in price based on the trench results, a little caution is called for. Many of these well-positioned drill holes often miss; the grocery money should not be riding on such a situation.

DRILLING & DRILL RESULTS

The proof is in the drilling! A lot of the safest, biggest money made on mining stocks is through the correct interpretation of drill results. This is especially true when the general market is not trading at a feverish pitch and near its all time high valuation records as this one is. In quieter times, several good drill holes might escape the attention of the general public, giving the astute investor an opportunity to evaluate the situation and take advantage of it. Today, with everyone on the edge of their chair, waiting for a chance to jump on the first sign of a new discovery, this luxury of time is not available. Companies even rumored to have good drill results now see their stock prices quickly rise to levels well above what a careful evaluation of the data would indicate reasonable. To cope with present market conditions it is necessary to calculate the value of the results, then decide if the active market premium added to the stock price is worth paying.

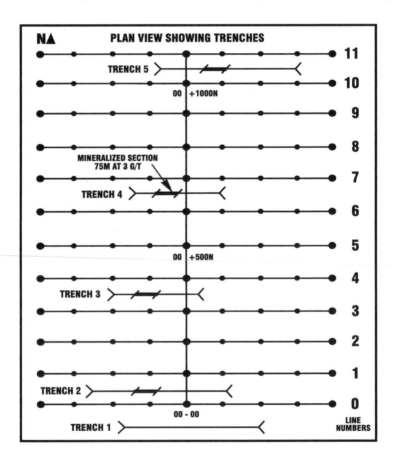

This article will not make you an expert at calculating ore reserves or establishing their exact dollar value. That's what the engineering companies and senior mining analysts do. They have all the current information, reams of historical data, years of experience, personnel, time, and computer programs to assist them. Rather, it will enable you to spot important developments early and come up with ballpark evaluations. Once you identify an interesting situation, my advice is to check it out with your multiple sources of information. Within half a dozen telephone calls you will find someone close to the situation. That lead will turn into another, then another; soon you will know as much as anyone does about the company and the project. When contemplating a serious investment based on real numbers, you should utilize every possible source of information available.

To visualize drill hole data, it must be seen in a cross sectional format. That is illustrated in the diagram on the next page. It depicts a cross sectional view of four drill holes, all drilled at different angles, 2 from the 100N+200E and 2 from the 100N+500E marker on the grid. These holes were drilled to the west to intersect a mineralized zone in the vicinity of and running parallel to the base line. Holes 1, 2, and 3 hit the zone at different angles and returned different length intersections grading on average 3 grams gold per tonne. The true width of the zone must be used to calculate tonnage. It is different than the length of the mineralized intersection in the drill core and is usually noted in the news release. If not, it can be obtained from the company. In this simplified illustration the average true width from the three drill intersections averages out to be 150 meters. Hole number 4 did not hit the zone, indicating a vertical depth limitation (cut off) of 250 meters for the zone.

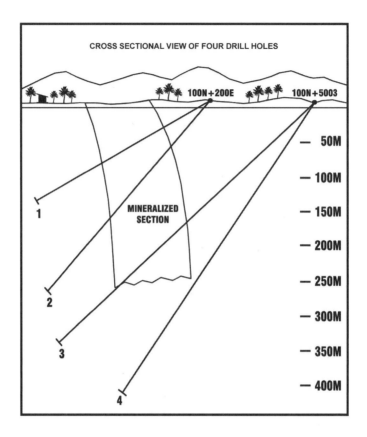

Let's assume a similar set of four holes were drilled from the same easterly locations on grid lines 400N and 1100N, and they returned similar results. It would be reasonable to project a zone of mineralization averaging 3 grams gold per tonne, over an average true width of 150 meters to a vertical depth of 250 meters—for a strike length (distance) of 1,000 meters (the distance from line 100N to line 1100N on the base line). With these numbers you can calculate the zone's and the stock's value. The math is the same as for anomalies and trenches. **1,000m length X 150m width X 250m projected depth X 2.6 conversion factor = 97.5 million tonnes X 0.0965 oz/t grade (3g/t÷ 31.1035 g/t oz) = 9.4 million contained ounces gold X US$25 value of one ounce in the ground = US$235.2 million value X**

1.10 US/CDN exchange rate = CDN$258.7 million value ÷ 10 million shares issued = CDN$25.87 per share.

In all the above monetary calculations, I have used the *'present day value of the metal in the ground approach'* to estimate value. There are other methods, but none of them are as quick or reliable for our purposes. This approach is **extremely change sensitive** to the price used for the metal in the ground. Published data on recent sales of mineral reserves indicate that drill-proven gold reserves in the ground from non-producing properties had been selling from US$40 to US$70 per ounce, with the average being around US$50. Very recent acquisitions suggest that major companies are willing to pay much higher prices ($75–$125 per ounce gold) for early stage reserve estimates. Gold reserves from producing properties are selling well over US$125 per ounce. The way to use this data is to run the calculation with various gold prices. The more you do it, the more the averages start to make sense to you. If US$50 had been used instead of US$25 in the last value calculation, the value of the stock would have been CDN$51.74 per share rather than CDN$25.87.

SUMMARY—WHAT TO LOOK FOR

Major mining companies are willing to pay more than investors for junior companies in order to acquire their reserves. Therefore, identifying potential takeover targets early has proven to be a very profitable investment strategy. Keep in mind that is exactly what you are trying to do and exactly what the information in **How Much Is That** is designed for. The majors are interested in high-grade, high-profit-margin deposits and those with the potential to contain very large reserves. Applying the tools in **How Much Is That** to each company you are interested in will quickly enable you to identify those with properties that are substantially above or below the average. Although the results can vary greatly, using them will aid you in making investment decisions from early stage exploration programs through the development of a major ore deposit.

Brian Fagan is the editor and publisher of Stocks and Speculations—an international forum for stock speculators specializing in natural resource, energy, and special situation opportunities. Please visit www.StocksandSpeculations.com for more information. All copyright reserved by Brian Fagan.

10

Australian Mining Stocks: What You Need to Know about the Currency, Economy, Mining Districts, and Australian Stock Exchange Before You Invest

Neil Charnock

There is a wide range of factors to consider when successfully investing in junior gold stocks. If you don't want to blow your money you had better study books like this one very carefully and listen to what contributors have to say as well. I will try to condense years of experience and a massive amount of data into a brief on the subject and readers would be well advised to study the various points made until you understand what we are talking about. If not, then you may be gambling and not investing, which decreases your chances of winning in what can be a very profitable endeavor. Juniors are both the hardest to get right and also the most lucrative if you do. They are unproven, yet have the potential to grow by a much larger degree than any other sector. This is not for the feint hearted so if you want to play to win you have to get armed to the teeth with knowledge.

WHY OWN GOLD—FUNDAMENTALS OF GOLD AS LINKED TO MONEY AND BANKING

I hope you have heard of the story about how frogs can be lulled to sleep in a pot of water. Apparently these beautiful little creatures can be fooled this way if you start them in cool water and turn up the heat very slowly. After they fall asleep in the warming water, the temperature can be gradually raised until they can be boiled to death, which is disgusting of course. Worse still this is a useful metaphor for the treatment of the working masses under a fiat monetary system. The term fiat means un-backed currency, generally this means un-backed by gold. People are not frogs so we just vote out governments when financial conditions get too upsetting for us. Unfortunately, this does not help because governments are not directly the cause, nor do they do anything to change it either.

The very core operation of the modern monetary system is the problem. It is inflationary and always will be because it is debt based and does not create the interest it demands of the borrowers. Yes that's right . . . the debt is basically created "out of thin air" through borrowing/lending and this has to be paid back with interest; however, the interest is not created. So for the money plus interest to be paid back this fiat debt/money monster has to grow in an endless inflationary cycle through the increasingly rapid creation of more money. The ever-greater pool of liquidity (money/credit) allows for the removal of the interest and debt repayments without creating a rapid collapse; this is equivalent to the water slowly warming. The basis of this system, which ironically disconnected from the gold standard, is extremely positive for gold and silver, which will always be closely connected. It is positive for the precious metals because it relies on inflation to survive in itself; this puts upward pressure on metal prices. This is worth putting another way. Paper money, created without the backing of a promise to pay in gold as it was under the gold standard, relies on confidence in the paper (now plastic) it is printed on. It relies on trust in the system of government and their economic management that backs the paper money in the absence of gold which requires no trust. Gold is as "good as gold" as the old saying goes.

The un-backed or government-backed paper money can be created in any quantity. However, if the rate of this creation is too rapid, trust and confidence will erode and gold will start to rise rapidly out of fear. Therefore gold price behavior acts as an economic barometer of potentially unstable economic conditions and can sound alarm bells so a rapidly rising gold price is counter to the interests of the current banking system. It "cramps their style" or business ambitions, which are to create as much money as the market can bear. Yet the inflationary nature of fiat money lights a fuse under gold sooner or later as debt levels rise to unsustainable levels and imbalances get out of control in the whole economic system. We saw round one of this for the modern era through the second half of the 1970s and this will happen again.

ECONOMIC CONDITIONS IN 2007

The current imbalances (just to name a few) are:

- Debt levels are worse than at the end of the 1920s as com-pared as a percentage to gross domestic product (GDP), mature Western economies with comparatively little re-maining manufacturing capacity (it migrated to Asia).
- Mountains of foreign reserves in Asia looking to diversify out of the U.S. dollar.
- Asset bubbles created by easy money and extremely low interest rates such as shares, property and bonds.
- Last, but not least, are the derivatives markets that have mushroomed in parabolic fashion to somewhere in the re-gion of $400,000,000,000,000. That's 400 trillion dollars of interconnected paper contracts that threaten the entire eco-nomic system as we know it. Four hundred trillion is

roughly 30+ times the total U.S. GDP! This is uncharted territory.

A series of large defaults, perhaps resulting from just one or two, in this paper house of cards, has the capacity to bring on serious chaos within the financial system causing a panic even greater than in 1929. If you tried to go back to the gold standard with the current amount of money in the U.S. financial system alone, we would need a gold price of over $30,000 per ounce to cover it all. As astute investors and the newly affluent Asians wake up to what is happening, in ever increasing numbers the competition for this tiny hoard of exceptionally rare metal will be fierce. If, or some say when, we do get into a crisis of no return due to all of the problems listed above and others I did not have space to mention, then the rush for the stability, plus protection of gold and silver, will be fear driven and extreme.

This introduction is far from complete and deserves a book on its own so I cannot possibly cover the full scope and range of these issues in this contribution. We try to cover this kind of education at scale on our web site and provide the right mix of information in our data products. Obtaining accurate information through all the hype can save you a massive amount of time. This in turn allows the average investor to broaden their knowledge across the whole sector so they can in turn make more informed decisions about which stocks to put on a short list for further research . . . perhaps leading to their own decision to invest.

SUPPLY VS. DEMAND

The truly insignificant amount of gold ever mined and the even smaller available amount of silver will simply not go around when the music stops. If you can imagine a solid cube with sides approximately 22 meters long—then you can imagine all the gold ever mined. Australia is particularly interesting, 8 out of the top 10 largest gold nuggets ever found were discovered here and we are a global top four gold mining nation. We hold roughly

10% of current known global un-mined resources with 5,225 tonnes. Significant new supply from global mining is not on the horizon and the large global gold miners have had difficulty replacing reserves or their own stock of gold. Traditionally, these majors have required very large projects to justify their investment and time. They wanted economy of scale. I wonder when this will change to smaller and smaller deposits. Will it be when gold gets more expensive than $1,000 per ounce, or perhaps $2,000?

AUSSIE GOLD STOCK PERFORMANCE SO FAR IN THE GOLD BULL MARKET

The major gold miners rose from a very low base in 2000 and have strong gains although nothing compared to North America because of exchange rates. We saw one preliminary run in the junior gold miners back in the second half of 2003 and into early 2004, many have even fallen back to pre-rally levels since then . . . rock bottom. Activity amongst the juniors has been increasing over the second half of 2006 and into early 2007. Activity tends to occur before major rallies and can last for several months before they launch into a broad rally through the junior sector. Here is the really interesting thing though . . . although the gold bull started in 2001 in the USA, the price has only broken key resistance at AUD$580 per ounce in Australia (as from August 2005). Yes that's right, the gold bull just started in terms of our dollar in Australia in 2005 even though activity among the miners has been increasing considerably the last few years in response to global trends. The smaller juniors usually respond in the later stages of a gold rally and this is important to keep in mind. Readers will have to seek a guide on where this sector is at when this text is read . . . where in the cycle does this compute now in real time as you read this?

SO WHAT NOW (2007) FOR AUSTRALIAN PRECIOUS METALS MINERS?

The first thing to understand is all of the above. The second thing to put together in this picture is that the scramble to buy protective metals will spill over into demand for the shares in the related gold mining companies all over the globe. At some point buyers will be after any gold stock, just like during the final stages of the dot-com boom. However, fear is far more powerful than greed . . . this will be bigger. As of March 2007, this has not happened yet.

Wealthy investors and the astute aside, I see huge demand for the quality projects within the junior sector from large and even mid-tier mining companies. When the average investor is informed of an economic crisis on the television and in the major newspapers, they will start to catch on. After some time the rally will cause a contagion (spreading) of demand across the whole gold/silver sector. This may even spread to "dog stocks," or "holes in the ground with a liar on top." These are to be avoided at all cost in my opinion, so I have included some data to assist you to avoid this.

SELECTING JUNIOR RESOURCE STOCKS: MANAGEMENT

Fortunately, the long bear market caused many large companies to down size their exploration teams and so many quality staff have ended up in the junior companies. Finding quality management and geologists is the first key to selection and I look at what these professionals have done in the past. Past performance in identification, delineation, finance, and development of operational mines, is essential. I prefer a mix of geologists and hardcore industry professionals, such as former operations managers and the like to make up the majority of management.

REPORTING AND EXPLORATION

Management is responsible for reporting and potential investors have to understand the difference of importance/significance between rock chip sampling and JORC compliant resources. Briefly the JORC Code is designed to ensure transparent and standardized reporting of resources by publicly identified competent persons as defined by the Code.

In grass roots exploration, a geologist scours prospective ground looking for special rock samples; this is obviously part of the training so they are not going to bring back useless sample material. The rock may have also been transported over distances so it may not represent what lies under the surface—just an indication of what might be. High-grade results from this level of activity are not even slightly conclusive. However, in conjunction with other indications, it may be of interest.

Shallow drilling will follow interesting grass roots exploration and then, if results warrant, this will be followed by wide spaced deeper drilling. Whilst this can be an exciting phase, be aware that a well-publicized drill result in isolation is no indication of a viable deposit. Be wary of how these kinds of results are reported. Closer spaced drilling will follow if further financing through share dilution helps keep the drills turning. Finance is usually raised by the issue of new shares in the junior sector as they do not have the funds required for long expensive and comprehensive drill programs required to prove their resources.

JORC CODE AND PROJECT FINANCE

You want to see closer drill spacing, diagrams and resource modeling to show promise. In order for a project to go to production it will need to convince lenders to advance considerable funds. The banks or venture capitalists will want to see delineation (complete identification) of a viable resource which means close spaced drilling and a JORC compliant estimate of Measured resources (highest level of confidence) or at least with a mixture of Indicated resources. A lower certainty measurement is Inferred resources.

The market will generally judge and value companies with the highest potential resources by size and with one other consideration on this level, which is grade. The grade of the deposit will largely contribute to the likelihood of development because this will show long term potential. Lower grade deposits may look attractive during price spikes. If they are large enough and near surface with low stripping ratios, they might even be viable in normal commodity price conditions. Stripping ratio refers to how much material has to be removed before the company can get at the valuable ore. Higher grade near surface deposits that have necessary scale will produce the larger price gains as they are drilled. Higher grade underground resources can also be highly prized. There is more to the picture though . . .

DIVERSIFICATION

Gold is not commonly mined as the only activity of small or large companies. Gold is not commonly mined on its own either, often it is found with silver or copper. This can be a good thing in the riskier junior sector. Lack of capital and cash flow is one problem and specialization can be another if this one commodity drops in price. I have elected to invest in diversified miners that have interests in copper, zinc, nickel and other base metals or even uranium and this has worked well in the early stages of the general commodities bull market. Later on, I will move to investment in "gold or silver only" miners if and when conditions justify.

LOCATION, LOCATION, LOCATION

Mining can be like real estate in this sense. Australia mined about 250 tonnes (t) of gold in 2006. The Super Pit in Kalgoorlie, WA, produced 26t and dominated production. Australian production for the forth quarter of 2006 was 62t. Of this 62t, all in rounded numbers, 42t was mined in Western Australia (WA), 8t in New South Wales (NSW), 5t in Queensland (QLD), 4t Northern Territory (NT), 2t in Victoria (VIC), 1t each in Tasmania (TAS) and South Australia (SA).

Old mining districts that have been under-explored by modern methods are excellent targets, so are mines within prolific districts or along known lines of geological lode. Australia is blessed with several excellent mining districts and gold occurrences tend to be found in these districts and along fairly well defined paths called corridors so this can be a promising guide to juniors and their prospects.

Major districts in Australia are: Kalgoorlie/Coolgardie, Leonora, Menzies, Ashburton, Pilbara, and Kemberley (WA). Included in the far southwest is the giant Boddington mine under construction. Also Bathurst, Hill End, Armidale, Orange, and generally right through the Lachlan Fold Belt (NSW). Then there is the Charters Towers, Gympie, Croydon, Mt Isa (QLD), the golden triangle Avoca—Castlemaine—Wedderburn plus Bendigo, Ballarat (central Vic.), Tanami, Pine Creek, McArthur River (silver) (NT). North West and central north Tasmania, Gawler Craton, and York Penninsula (SA).

Now you have narrowed down the juniors to excellent mining districts, perhaps in key states, along strike (down along a known mineralized corridor) from established mines or at least in similar geological setting to other economic deposits. Next issue is infrastructure. Is there access to the site, or rail if necessary, power nearby, or available staff? Apart from a deposit being of a viable size all this can make or break the ability of a small company being able to secure finance to develop a deposit. If all the right elements are in place you have a winner and the market gets excited driving up the share price. Of course the world and mining is grey and not black and white. So a strong weighting of positive factors along with an absence of black or really negative factors is well sought after.

SPECIAL SITUATIONS

Thanks to the long bear market from 1980 to 2000, there are some juniors who have been able to buy old mines with infrastructure in place. A mill, tailings dams, perhaps a decline or tunnel down to deeper resources, an accommodation village, power grid, and roads can be a huge time and cost savings not always reflected in the share price of a junior. Sometimes the old mine waste called a mullock heap or tailings can be lucrative enough to put through with higher grade ore because it will be right next to the mill and requires no blasting to win it from the earth. The time taken to bring a project to fruition—production, profits and finally dividends, can take nearly a decade. The special situation stocks can jump ahead of this process.

FINAL SELECTION OF A JUNIOR INVESTMENT AND TIMING

My strategy is to look for a range of juniors that have sound and proven management, which may be somewhat conservative. Special situations as described above in proven mineral districts and with proven resources are a favorite. Diversification is a bonus and then I look for a reasonable level of finance so that I do not have to suffer through numerous dilution periods where shares are issued to raise capital in final preparation for production. At times they have strong joint venture partnerships that finance the project at various capital raising stages. Exciting deposits of scale are also a favorite, particularly if they are in a district that is generating positive news and results. Of course investing in a hot stock will mean that the sector is also hot and this will be the case in gold stocks down the track. You may have picked up this book when everybody is chasing stocks in the gold sector, which will mean you have to follow these considerations carefully to find the right companies for your precious investment capital. Those that get in early can look to buy with considerable leverage.

One strategy I like to employ is to buy in and really hit a key stock or two and hold for the longer term. I like to buy during a base formation on the chart and add purchases on price pull backs while I accumulate vastly undervalued special situations. On minor price spikes I can lighten up if I wish. What I really aim to do here is to wait patiently until there is a considerable price spike where the true value of the company is recognized by the market. This will maximize returns through leverage. As price surges I can then sell a portion of these companies and reinvest or diversify into different assets if appropriate. The point is to get back initial capital and healthy investment returns and to hold a portion for the final blow off spikes that lay ahead in gold.

The next important strategy is to invest as the sector gets hot. The old saying 'all boats float in a rising tide' rings true in this instance. In the last few years it has been uranium stocks and of late any grass roots stage company has done well with the exception of the dog stocks. A really hot sector will push the juniors higher as explained earlier. Choose according to the fundamental parameters included when this time comes for potentially stellar profits.

Finally there is the timing aspect. We try to provide a range of quality technical analysis education on our web site to assist investors. For those not familiar with or able to devote the time to learn charting and the art of technical analysis, we plan to provide a range of timing services. Entry points are important particularly when the rally really kicks in. Nothing goes up in a straight line and even hot stocks and the pullbacks in price can upset investors into taking losses. Learn about timing and technical analysis to increase your chances of success.

TAKING YOUR REWARDS

Greed is going to be a factor in future just like during the dot-com boom. One must have an exit strategy because these stocks are not a buy and hold for the long term. They are a buy/sell so don't forget to reward yourself by taking partial profits at the appropriate time. You should be looking to do a fair share of this along the way and even reduce your investment in these stocks when everybody loves the sector. Long-term rallies go on much longer than most people expect, however, they do not last forever. At the end of the day it can be wiser to leave room for somebody else to make a profit rather than expecting to exit at the top. Remember many investors bought gold and silver during the 1970s and forgot to sell, losing all their profits in the 20-year bear market that followed.

Personally, I will be trading on a short term basis when this really heats up to a point where every man and his dog has been making a fortune from gold and silver stocks. This is a totally different strategy to what I am describing in this essay, as the special situations and easy money will be gone. Then it will come down to the other data provided and timing. I strongly recommend investors learn about technical analysis and the different time frames of investment rather than sticking to just one, which may not be appropriate in different conditions. One last point—it will be my physical bullion that gets sold last in the precious metals bull market, as I then seek the next undervalued asset class.

Neil Charnock is the owner/editor of GoldOz.com. For information on mining, Australian geology, related stocks, technical analysis, how to buy ASX–Australian stocks, data and basic timing services, please visit www.GoldOz.com.au.

11

World Class Deposits: Why You Should Study Past Winners

Kevin Corcoran

Some say drill results are an exploration company's truth serum. Company promoters can tell you about their strategic land holdings, experienced management team and point to their Vancouver office address, but the only thing that matters is what's in the ground. The cost of running a mine varies greatly by country and geographical region. There are numerous factors that account for the cost of production including labor, government and taxes, joint venture agreements, infrastructure, depth, type of deposit (host rock), and extraction method.

Other economic considerations include the amount and concentration of metal, cost of refining and the market value of the metal. To be of commercial grade, for example, the following metals must be concentrated in the amounts indicated (this excludes minerals mined as byproducts): aluminum, about 30%; iron, 30+%; copper, 0.6–1%; lead, 2–4%; zinc, 3–8%; and gold, silver, and uranium, only a small fraction of a percent.

Thankfully, you don't need to know the exact costs of all these variables. But it is very important to study world-class mining operations. Begin to learn about different ore bodies, grades and the regions they lie in, and you'll begin to better understand what stocks the market will favor. The earlier you find companies that offer the greatest potential to develop an ore body or be taken over, the greater your leverage and profit.

Here is a list of world class mines of past and present. Remember, 3 out of 4 major discoveries are made by juniors.

Barrick's Goldstrike property on the Carlin Trend, NV
Open pit: 105,206,000 tons
Gold average grade: 3.9 grams/ton (g/t), or
0.143 troy ounces per ton (opt)
Estimated 13 million ounces contained
1.5 million ounces produced in 2005
Cost per ounce: US$255

Goldstrike underground: 7,662,000 tons
Gold average grade 11.5 g/t, or 0.37 opt
Estimated 2.8 million ounces contained
510,000 ounces produced in 2005
Cost per ounce: US$255

Freeport Mcmoran's Grasberg Mine has open pit,
underground mines and four concentrators
Papua, Indonesia
46 million ounces of gold estimated
Gold: 0.5–2 g/t, or 0.016–0.064 opt
Copper: 1.2–1.5% average grade

Newmont's Golden Giant surface and underground mine
Ontario, Canada
Ended "official" operation in 2005
Gold: 10 g/t, or 0.3 opt
6 million ounces gold over 21 years

Goldcorp's Dickensen/Red Lake Mine: 1948–Present
Ontario, Canada
9.4 million tons milled
Gold: 19.8 g/t, or 0.638 opt
5.9 million ounces produced

Gold Fields' South African operations in the
Witwatersrand Basin:

Driefontein: (surface and underground)
Gold average grade: 5.2 g/t combined
1.2 million ounces produced in 2006
Cost per ounce: US$355

Kloof: (surface and underground)
Gold average grade: 7.8 g/t combined
914,000 ounces produced in 2006
Cost per ounce: US$421

Beatrix: (surface and underground)
Gold average grade: 5.2 g/t combined
596,000 ounces produced in 2006
Cost per ounce: US$409

Silver Wheaton (contracted silver holding company):

San Dimas Mine (underground), Durango/Sinaloa, Mexico
4.31 million tonnes
Proven/Probable silver reserves: 53.8 million ounces
388.2 g/t, or 12.48 opt
9.5 million ounces produced in 2006

Yauliyacu Mine, Peru
3.16 million tonnes
Proven/Probable silver reserves: 13.1 million ounces
129.2 g/t, or 4.15 opt
Silver Wheaton's contract is for 4.75 million ounces total, though
it produces 3.5 million ounces of silver annually

Note: Goldcorp owns the San Dimas and Yauliyacu mines and
produces silver as a byproduct that is sold to Silver Wheaton at a
fixed cost (usually under market).

Silver Standard:

La Colorada Mine, Zacatecas/Durango, Mexico
Proven/Probable silver reserves: 19.8 million ounces
470 g/t, or 15.11 opt
2006 production:
Silver: 3.5 million ounces at cash cost per ounce of US$6.49
Gold: 3,501 ounces
Lead: 153 tonnes

Huaron Mine (underground), Peru
Proven/Probable silver reserves: 51.3 million ounces
167 g/t, or 5.38 opt
2006 production:
Silver: 3.7 million ounces at cash cost per ounce of US$2.41
Gold: 1,832 ounces
Lead: 6,858 tonnes
Copper: 1,603 tonnes
Zinc: 6,858 tonnes

San Vicente Mine (open pit), Bolivia
Proven/Probable silver reserves: 18.8 million ounces
315.6 g/t, or 10.15 opt
Production in 2006:
Silver: 264,573 ounces at cash cost per ounce of US$3.49
Copper: 52 tonnes
Zinc: 805 tonnes
Silver Standard has 55% ownership

Rio Tinto's Bingham Canyon Mine
Southwest of Salt Lake City, Utah
Open pit porphyry copper deposit—world's largest man made
excavation at 0.75 miles deep, 2.5 miles wide
As of end–2003 reserves at:
28,000,000 tons
Copper: 0.56%

Gold: 0.35 g/t
Silver: 3.16 g/t

CVRD Inco's Voisey's Bay nickel mine
Newfoundland/Labrador, Canada
One of the world's largest nickel deposits
Proven/Probable nickel reserves: 4.97 billion lbs, or
141 million tonnes at 1.6% nickel
110 million lbs of nickel produced annually
Copper: 0.14%

Xstrata's Kidd underground base metals mine,
Ontario, Canada
One of the world's largest volcanic massive sulphide deposits
Began operation in 1966
Estimated 24.4 million tonnes:
Copper: 2.90%
Zinc: 5.77%
Lead: 0.25%
Silver: 75 g/t, or 2.14 opt

Impala Platinum's Merensky Mine (underground)
Bushveld, South Africa
135 million tonnes:
Platinum: 2.7 g/t, 21.6 million ounces contained
Palladium: 1.19 g/t, 5.2 million ounces
Ruthenium: 0.39 g/t, 1.7 million ounces
Rhodium: 0.214 g/t, 929,700 ounces
Iridium: 0.086 g/t, 372,000 ounces
Gold: 0.176 g/t, 764,000 ounces

Brinex's Kitts and Michelin uranium mines
Labrador, Canada:

Kitts Mine discovered 1956
184,957 tonnes:

U308: 0.73%, or 16.09 lbs per tonne
Total historical resources: 2,976,240 lbs

Michelin Mine discovered 1968
6,426,095 tonnes:
U308: 0.13%, or 2.87 lbs per tonne
Total historical resources: 18,417,412 lbs

Cameco's Cigar Lake (production expected 2010)
Saskatchewan, Canada, in the Athabasca Basin
Proven/Probable reserves: 226.3 million pounds of uranium
U308: 21%, or an amazing 420 lbs per ton
Cameco's share: 113.2 million pounds

Cameco's McArthur River
Saskatchewan, Canada, in the Athabasca Basin
World's largest, high grade uranium deposit
Proven/Probable reserves: 367 million pounds of uranium
U308: 20.5%
Cameco's share: 256 million pounds

BHP Billiton's Olympic Dam Mine (underground)
Central South Australia
Began operation in 1988
Uranium grade and reserves:
0.06%: 60,200 tonnes
0.05%: 540,780 tonnes
0.04%: 480,000 tonnes
0.03%: 442,000 tonnes
Currently produces around 5,000 tonnes (11 million lbs) of
uranium oxide and 210,000 tonnes (463 million lbs) of copper
per year

Heathgate Resources' Beverley Mine, South Australia
Began operation in 2000
1,166,666 tonnes:

U308: 0.18%
Currently produces 1,000 tonnes (2.2 million lbs) of uranium
oxide per year
15–30 year mine life, in-situ leach (ISL) recovery

Phelps Dodge's Henderson Mine (underground)
Empire, Colorado
Molybdenum: 0.0024% (various grades throughout)
Processes up to 30,000 tons a day
Largest primary producer of molybdenum in the world
In operation since 1976 and has processed 160 million tons
of ore and 770 million pounds of molybdenum
during a 27 year period

Samarco's Alegria iron ore mine (open pit)
Minas Gerais, Brazil
BHP Billiton and CVRD each own 50% of Samarco
Proven/Probable reserves: 515 million tonnes
Iron ore average grade: 44.93%
Annual production as of 2005: 20.9 Mt/y

CBG's Sangaredi, Bidikoum and Silidara bauxite (aluminum
ore) open pit mines, Guinea, West Africa
Alcoa and Alcan each hold a large stake in CBG
Proven reserves at 2,300 million tonnes
Historical bauxite grades:
Sangaredi: 56–58%
Bidikoum: 50%
Silidara: 52%

Cambior's Omai Bauxite Mine (open pit)
Guyana, South America
Proven/Probable reserves at 62 million tonnes
Bauxite grading: 60%

12

Oh, Canada!

Know the Secret to This Country's Mining Success

Dr. Russell McDougal

When many investors think of Canada, the first thing that comes to mind is the abundance of natural resources. Canada has natural resources like Florida has grains of sand and Texas has oil. It's no surprise that the Canadian economy is largely resource based. Canada has developed and nurtured an entire exploration and production infrastructure over the centuries. They have schools, institutions, markets and vast financial resources all dedicated to take advantage of their resource heritage. It is nothing short of phenomenal. What you may be surprised to learn is that they have taken this resource expertise to a global level.

Our northern neighbors haven't been content to stay home and ply their trades only in their own country. They are more adventuresome than that. "Canadian know-how" has left few areas of the earth unexplored. They search for silver in Mexico and South America, gold in China, platinum in South Africa, diamonds in Namibia, oil in Indonesia, iron in Sweden . . . well, you get the picture. These guys are beyond good! Quite frankly, the Canadians are the world's experts in the field of resource exploration and your opportunity lies alongside theirs.

The global economy is expanding rapidly and putting strains on most commodity supplies. Get used to it. Trees don't grow to the sky, but they certainly can grow very big (check out the Redwoods of Western Canada). As an intelligent investor, you will want to have exposure to this secular bull market trend over the coming years. If you want leveraged speculation in exploration you will want to delve into the arena of Canadian micro-cap companies. You may be surprised to learn that it is the talented, mobile and efficient junior mining companies that make the most resource discoveries, not the majors like Newmont or Barrick that most people are familiar with. You needn't look for these companies on the NYSE because they're not there. Their home typically starts out on the Toronto Venture Exchange or the Toronto Exchange itself. As success comes their way they will seek listings on the NASDAQ Pink Sheets, the NASDAQ or the American Stock Exchange.

The goal is to invest in the most promising companies when they are quite small. A trusted source long ago said, "Give some money to good people and very often they will discover something." This sounds simple but it is actually quite profound. You stack the deck in your favor when you can tap into the talent pool of 'good people'. That's the key, not the size of the company. Don't make the mistake of thinking relative smallness in a company is a bad thing. There are innumerable thriving businesses with world class expertise that are too small for the big funds or institutional investors to get involved with. These are the companies with the potential to multiply in price once they start plying their trade and have exploration success. Of course, that's the point when we'll gladly sell shares to the 'big boys'.

There is another reason for buying Canadian: dollar diversification. No matter how widely diversified your investments are in different sectors of the economy, you are not truly diversified if everything you own is based on the US dollar. Please don't learn this lesson the hard way over the next 5 to 10 years. Canadian stocks that were purchased in 2003 were bought with an exchange rate of 69 cents US for each Canadian dollar (called the 'loonie'). Presently, it takes 92 cents US to purchase one Canadian dollar. In other words, even if your investments were flat during this period you would have still made around 30% in three years on currency appreciation alone. Not bad considering that would not have been the primary reason for buying the stocks.

I am convinced the US dollar has trouble baked deeply into its cake. On the other hand, countries with treasure troves of natural resources ordinarily experience currency appreciation during commodity bull markets. I believe the dollar and the loonie will likely see parity before too long. And considering the commodities super cycle we are currently in, I suggest the bull market in Canadian dollars still has many years to run.

You might be surprised how easy it is to set up a brokerage account that can efficiently buy Canadian stocks. I receive no consideration whatsoever for these recommendations, but I did want to pass along three brokerages that I have found to be exemplary:

1. Global Resource Investments 800–477–7853. (Full service brokerage house specializing in resources. Ask for Luke Smith or Ben Miller).

2. Charles Schwab & Co. 800–435–4000 (They have an efficient international investing department).

3. Pennaluna & Co. 800–535–5329 (Long established discount brokerage out of Idaho, with a special place in their hearts for mining stocks).

The bottom line . . . If you want to speculate in resource exploration stocks, Canada is truly a speculator's paradise.

13

How to Purchase Canadian and Australian Stocks Using Your Online Discount Broker

Kevin Corcoran

Canada's economy is driven by commodities. And because Canadians are known for their mining and exploration success at home and abroad, the world's most successful mining companies choose to list on the Toronto Stock Exchange and the TSX Venture. Sixty-two percent of the world's exploration companies list on the TSX–Venture Exchange—where many micro-cap exploration companies issue their IPO. Because of this concentration of liquidity, resource fund managers, private equity and mutual funds tend to focus their investments in Canada. Naturally, this is where you will want to put some of your capital to work.

In the United States, the SEC only allows U.S. investors to use 'licensed' Canadian brokers. For many Canadian online brokers, licensing is very expensive. This virtually eliminates the option to trade through a discount broker. So how can you gain access to the lucrative Canadian market? You can set up an account with a full service broker in the United States or Canada that is licensed to deal in the Canadian markets. But this isn't ideal for many of today's online investors who prefer to trade their accounts actively with minimal trading costs. However, there is a way to trade Canadian equities through your existing broker.

LOOKING UP AND PRICING CANADIAN MINING STOCKS

Junior mining and exploration companies listed on the Canadian stock exchange also have a corresponding 5-series alpha symbol that trades on the U.S. Over-the-Counter Pink Sheets market. When people think of Pink Sheets and OTC-listed companies, images of penny stock scams come to mind. These are **not** "Pink Sheets" stocks. When an order is executed on the Pink Sheets, the same order is transacted on the Canadian exchange. The Pink Sheets market is only a means for American investors to access the Canadian markets. The 5-series ticker symbol is traded in US dollars and reflects the listed stock price on the Canadian exchange.

As part of the transaction, American investors must convert US dollars to Canadian dollars. Yahoo! Finance allows you to pull up a company's Canadian and Pink Sheets symbol (www.finance.yahoo.com). Let's say you'd like to buy 100 shares of Esperanza Silver Corporation. In Yahoo! Finance, click "Symbol Lookup" and type "Esperanza Silver" into the Name field and press enter. Two ticker symbols will appear:

EPZ.V   (CDNX=Venture Exchange)
ESPZF.PK   (Other OTC=Pink Sheets)

Obtain the current price from "EPZ.V." This price will be in Canadian dollars. Now you need to convert this to US dollars. Go back to the Yahoo! Finance homepage, locate and click on "Currency Converter" and find out what the exchange rate is between the Canadian and US dollar.

It will display something that looks like this:

1 <u>Can $</u>   = 0.9356 (US$)

So, 93.6 cents US converts to 1 Canadian dollar. Conversely, in the same example, it takes CDN$1.07 to get US$1. Currency rates change frequently, so always obtain a current exchange rate before doing your conversion. Now multiply 93.6 cents by the current share price of EPZ.V and you get the US dollar price to use for your limit order.

Let's say Esperanza Silver is trading at CDN$2 a share:

0.936 X 2 = US$1.87

$1.87 is your current price in US dollars. Use the Pink Sheets symbol ESPZF when placing your online order and enter a limit price of $1.87 for 100 shares to get filled at the market. Do not use the "ESPZF" Pink Sheets-listed price. It only represents the last trade in the U.S. and is most likely inaccurate. Of course you can place your limit order below $1.87 depending on your investing strategy. Note: Not all U.S. online brokers allow you to place OTC Pink Sheets orders online. However, in some cases, your broker may not be aware of trading Canadian equities through the OTC Pink Sheets market. Call or email your broker for further information.

If you want to participate in the secular bull market in natural resources, it is critical that you understand how to convert Canadian dollars to US dollars to correctly execute limit orders. This same method can also be used for Australian mining stocks listed on the Australian Stock Exchange (go to Yahoo! Australia and New Zealand: www.au.finance.yahoo.com). Become proficient at this procedure and you'll be on your way to investing in Canadian and Australian-listed mining and exploration stocks.

If you prefer the support of a full service broker, find as many licensed brokers as possible and examine their credentials, fee structure and service plan before opening an account. Start with the "brokers" section at www.StingyInvestor.com. You can also go to www.NASDR.com to research potential brokers. Click on "Check Broker/Adviser Info," "NASD Public Disclosure Program," then "Perform an Online Search." After entering the name of the brokerage firm, you will receive a report listing the private and regulatory legal actions against the firm (if any).

14

Strategies for Junior Mining Stock Speculation

Clif Droke

I'm often asked what are some good resources to learn the fundamentals of junior mining stock investing and penny mining stock speculation. Unfortunately, there is precious little among the massive body of printed financial literature available today that deals specifically with the mining sector and the analysis of mining securities in particular (especially the junior golds). Thankfully, however, there are a handful of valuable books available to those who want to learn the basics of junior stock investing. One such resource is the somewhat dated, but still extremely useful book by Robert Bishop entitled, *The Investor's Guide to Penny Mining Stocks*. Published in 1987, this volume contains a wealth of information on the basics of the junior mining sector in general including an overview of the exploration and mining process. It also contains numerous valuable tips for picking the right low-priced mining shares for maximum profit, both for growth-oriented and conservative-minded investors.

Bishop begins his explanation of penny stock speculation principles in the junior mining sector by noting, ". . .it remains essential to understand that all mining stocks are at the mercy of the price of the commodity being sought, developed or mined." This is an important starting consideration for any investor in the junior mining stock sector to consider up front. If you as a prospective investor believe that the gold price is headed higher, then the junior mining stocks would be an excellent leverage tool for profiting from this expected rise in gold's price. Bishop adds to this basic observation by noting, "Aside from an appreciation that gold stocks are at the mercy of the gold price, having a well-defined point of view on the price trends of precious metals will help dictate both the degree of commitment and the timing of purchases and sales of penny mining shares. Having a philosophy on gold also makes it easier to take action at the appropriate time—or to weather the periodic price adversity that is common to all markets, sometimes especially so in the case of gold."

Bishop further adds that having an opinion on gold will also help determine whether mining stocks are held for the duration of a long bull market in precious metals, whether a trading strategy is adopted, or whether these markets are avoided altogether. The next most common question asked by the prospective junior mining stock investor is, "How much or what percentage of my capital should I allocate to a mining stock portfolio?" My own answer to that question is that it depends on the individual investor, namely, what is his emotional make-up when it comes to the financial markets (e.g., aggressive and risk-averse, or conservative and subject to being frightened by temporary pullbacks in share price).

I also advise my subscribers to only allocate that portion of their available discretionary capital to their portfolio that they feel they can afford to lose if worse absolutely comes to worse. Only commit those funds that are purely discretionary and not immediately needed for day-to-day business and personal survival. In a similar vein, Bishop writes, "It depends almost entirely on the person asking the question, his overall investment philosophy and its relation to current economic conditions and the investor's level of experience with the investment—whether it be gold, common stocks, junk bonds or rare coins." He adds, "I believe people should seek a comfort level and gain experience in the market. Based on that experience, the investor should work to develop a strategy that suits his financial and temperamental willingness to assume financial risk and perhaps more importantly, squares with his own track record in the market."

Bishop advises that just as precious metals mining stocks represent a segment of a larger portfolio, penny mining shares should occupy only a portion of a broadly diversified precious metals portfolio. At its core, that portfolio should consist of gold and silver bullion and blue-chip producers, says Bishop. "Like a pyramid rising from a base of security, more speculative issues should be added to a portfolio only after a conservative safety net is in place. At least some portion of the bullion is an insurance policy that should be held through thick and thin; beyond that 'insurance' position, the metals should be bought and sold based on changing economic conditions."

He opines that the blue-chip gold stocks are best suited to profit from cyclical advances in the price of gold. With respect to diversification Bishop adds, "Within the context of a precious metals portfolio, penny mining shares should represent a diversified group of companies. Mining is a game of bad odds, and owning shares in numerous companies reduces some of the inherent risks of mining stocks while at the same time increases the probability of rewards."

Penny mining shares are naturally much more speculative and volatile than blue-chip stocks of senior and mid-tier producers. They also tend to be highly seasonal from year-to-year. As such, they should normally represent a much smaller portion of the well-rounded precious metals portfolio. Nevertheless, there are times when it pays handsomely to be heavily long the low-priced junior golds. The big advantage to owning junior mining shares is that in times of a rising gold market they can out-perform the blue chips by hefty percentages. Knowing when such times are likely to begin is a subject addressed by Bishop in his book. "When everyone thinks alike, everyone is likely to be wrong" is the essence of the contrary opinion investment strategy advocated by Bishop. Humphrey B. Neill, who authored the preceding quotation, is generally regarded as the "father" of contrary opinion investing. The necessity of going against the crowd illustrates human nature at work, observes Bishop. It is also an example of crowd psychology that drives home what is easily the most important tenet of investing: Go against the crowd and you will be right more often than you will be wrong, he says.

For example, it was a timely move in 1980 to be a seller of silver when the infamous Hunt Brothers silver market corner debacle was at a peak and the wily brothers made the front pages of Time and Newsweek, as Bishop observed. It was also timely from a contrarian standpoint to later buy silver once again when the brothers were forced into filing bankruptcy years later. "The advantages of buying at market extremes are even more important in penny markets," says Bishop, "because these stocks are so much more volatile than bullion itself." As an example, Bishop noted that in the year his book was written the price of gold ranged from $378 to $482, a range of 27 percent. In contrast, the average stock of the junior mining shares at that time had a range of approximately 320 percent. "A contrary strategy rewards investors in any market, but because of the greater volatility of the penny shares, the rewards of true contrary investing are significantly more pronounced," writes Bishop.

Just as important as knowing when to buy is knowing when to sell. A strategy that Bishop strongly advocates is the sale of stocks that haven't performed to expectations. "The inability of many investors to bite the bullet, whether it be with stocks that aren't working out or merely aren't ripe with the same expectations they were at the time of purchase, is the reason many investors end up owning 25, 30, 50 or more companies," he writes. "These people buy companies and, rather than sell when things don't work out, relegate them to a kind of 'nonperforming' corner of a portfolio. Like old clothes in a closet that they hope to wear again, some investors file these stocks away in hopes that they'll come back to life."

Bishop goes on to address what is perhaps the most widely recognized strategy to take profits—by selling half of a stock position if it doubles in price. He dismisses this strategy as being "a sure way to instill mediocrity in a portfolio." Instead of this, he advises isolating the best stock in a portfolio, rather than arbitrarily selling half of what may turn out to be a stock that should have been held for much larger gains. He cites a study by the New York Stock Exchange that showed a stock that went up by 1,000 percent had 27 changes of ownership on the way up. Conversely, stocks that declined by the same percentage changed hands only twice on the way down. "The people in this example, at least, were cutting short their profits and letting their losses run—exactly the opposite of the way it's supposed to be done," observed Bishop. He urges taking partial profits at various times in a soaring stock, a sentiment that even the most aggressive traders should concur with. Bishop advises selling on a double "only if it squares with a short-term trading philosophy or your own ultra-conservative investment viewpoint."

PENNY MINING STOCK INVESTING

In his book, *The Investor's Guide to Penny Mining Stocks*, Bishop stresses the necessity of owning a diversified portfolio of penny mining shares. "Diversification," he points out, "spreads risk, thereby reducing them, and it also increases the odds of owning shares in a company whose shares skyrocket by 500 percent, 1,000 percent—or more." He adds, "Nobody knows what's going to be found underground until a property is drilled, and having several irons in the fire enhances the possibility that drilling results on at least one of a company's programs will be positive."

Taking the principle of diversification to the extreme, however, is one such "penny pitfall" that Bishop warns investors to avoid. Diversifying for the sake of diversification will not generate profits. A huge portfolio—especially one that isn't tended carefully, will mask the winners and even crowd them out with an abundance of underperformers. A timely selection of fundamentally and technically sound mining shares is the key ingredient to success in the junior mining sector.

Another pitfall of the over-diversification coin is that it tends to enrich one's broker at the investor's expense due to the higher commissions on smaller transactions, thus ensuring that investors never make a worthwhile profit. "Diversification is important," writes Bishop, "but it shouldn't preclude making serious money—not just the occasional big percentage gain that gets lost in the shuffle of a portfolio so large that it's almost impossible to follow anyway."

The flip side of the over-diversification coin is that too often investors don't own enough of the biggest winners in their portfolio. Bishop emphasizes that they should own stocks in a disproportionate amount based on their experience in the market and on their expectations for individual stocks. This is done to avoid being in the position of making huge gains in percentage points and only a negligible amount of money. "Investors who really like a stock . . . should also own more of it, not relegate it to a position of equality in a portfolio," he says.

Bishop concludes by stating, "Gold mining remains a speculative activity, but it's not the flagrant crap shoot it used to be. Barring a collapse of gold prices, choosing stocks with care and employing a contrary strategy to time purchases should produce profits much more often than losses."

Equally important in our discussion of penny mining investing is the practice of good portfolio management. In his excellent book, *Making Dollars With Pennies (How the Small Investor Can Beat the Wizards on Wall Street)*, author Max Bowser lists three basic rules for managing a well-selected penny stock portfolio. The first is quantity, i.e., how much of a given stock should the investor purchase.

Says Bowser, "Initially, you should take a small position [in a penny stock]. They do bounce around. Maybe they spike up for a transitory reason. Another newsletter or a brokerage firm recommends one of them. This is an artificial stimulus. "After a while they will settle back. You don't want to buy when they have spiked up. Improving performance is the only engine that drives up a stock price and keeps it up."

The second factor the investor needs to consider in portfolio management is time. As Bowser observes, time can be your best friend or your worst enemy. He points out that the liquidity of stocks in general (compared with other markets) often encourages investors to embrace a short-term view. "In fact," writes Bowser, "no other investment form has the liquidity of stocks. Because of this, many equity investors have unrealistic expectations. They want sensational results quickly. If a stock doesn't double in a year or two, they are ready to throw in the towel. They ignore the fact that it takes time for a company to develop." The lesson to be learned here is that above all, it requires patience to be a successful investor in the junior mining sector.

The third and final factor that Bowser relates to the successful speculation in penny stocks is that of discipline. "The chief advantage of having the discipline to follow a game plan is that it removes emotions from your decision making, especially in the critical area of selling. Which in many cases determines the success or failure of a portfolio."

For example, if a stock in your portfolio doubles and you sell half your position, you might be tempted to buy more shares on the next pullback of 25% to 35% from its previous high. But with penny stocks this is often not a wise thing to do since such sharp retracements are often the beginning of a decline and not merely a temporary pullback. Buying on the dips is a strategy that is usually best left to the larger cap stocks. As Bowser says, don't let "Mr. Greed" influence your emotions when investing in penny stocks.

WHAT TO BUY

Now let's discuss the mechanics of what to buy and how to identify the best mining companies based on fundamentals.

The merits of owning mining shares are many. In his classic book, *The Battle for Investment Survival*, Gerald Loeb made the following observation: "I think if one went to the trouble of reviewing the figures, one would find the better mines lived much longer than many corporations. One is very much more apt to extend an ore body than to find new sources of profit to bolster a perishing industry."

Loeb provides us with the rudiments to successful speculation in the mining sector in general. He asserts that despite the complexities involved with the gold and silver mining business, mining shares nevertheless have great interest and great value for those in a position to get the right information and evaluate it correctly. Loeb endorses investment in mining shares of companies with proven ore bodies and established reputations. He writes, "I feel the best ones are more attractive than general investment trusts and that appraisal of mines is more certain than appraisal of industrial or other prospects." (Paraphrased) He notes that the specialization of gold mining companies is likely to hold an additional advantage: "The frequency of granting options in mining finance is often the source of really huge and unexpected profits, very often out of all proportion to risks."

Loeb praises gold mining shares as coming nearest to the perfect means of preserving current purchasing power for future use, viz., the hoarding of metallic gold where it is legal. "Gold companies are relieved of any effort to find markets for their product in contrast with the usual extensive and costly sales departments of ordinary business concerns. Furthermore, the price of gold has broadly increased for centuries." He adds that gold shares are devaluation hedges and that "the desire for gold is the most universal and deeply rooted commercial instinct of the human race."

Now that the groundwork has been laid establishing the investment value of gold mining shares, let's take a look at the fundamental requirements for purchasing shares of gold mining companies. In *Making Dollars With Pennies*, R. Max Bowser lists several factors that must be considered for a prospective penny stock purchase. These requirements can be applied to junior mining stocks as well.

The first factor to consider when purchasing junior mining or other gold shares is a company's book value, which is roughly defined as being the difference between all of a company's assets and its liabilities, dividing the resulting figure by the number of common shares. According to Bowser, if the book value of a company is equal to or more than the price of its stock, it's a positive and that is the first step in the consideration of which shares to accumulate in the penny mining stock sector. Charles Allmon of the Growth Stock Outlook newsletter once wrote, "If I had to limit my stock selection to only one thing, I would choose book value."

Another prime factor to consider when trying to decide which penny mining shares to accumulate, is the highest price per share in the last two years. Writes Bowser, "The objective of our system is to have at least each purchase double in value . . . so we would like to know that at least once in the last two years it has been double its current price." He adds that on average, if an issue has performed well in the past it is most likely to repeat.

Another basic requirement for selecting penny mining shares is average daily trading volume. The more actively traded a stock is, the more liquid it is and hence easier to dispose of when the time comes to take profits. Make sure that you, as an investor, select a penny mining stock that has a fair average daily trading volume that indicates the stock is in demand, otherwise you may be stuck with shares that no one wants when you are trying to sell. Along with this consideration is the number of shares outstanding, which should never be excessive when compared with a company's annual sales.

Another factor that Bowser likes to look at when evaluating penny shares is the current ratio on the company's balance sheet. In fact, he considers it one of the most important facets of his personal rating system. This is defined as the relationship be-tween current assets and current liabilities. The minimum that

Bowser accepts is a ratio of 1.8 to 1, which means that for every $1.80 of current assets, there is $1.00 of current liabilities. In short, the ratio must be 1.8 to 1 or higher to warrant consideration for purchase.

Long-term debt is the next important factor to consider when evaluating low-priced shares. "Excessive long-term debt is an albatross," writes Bowser. "Every year interest has to be paid on it, plus part of the principal. And, these expenditures are considered a cost of doing business, so that they are deducted before taxes and thus reduce the amount of earnings available for per-share computations." Bowser maintains that if the long-term debt is more than 10% of a company's annual sales, it is excessive and does not warrant purchase of its shares.

Another important consideration when evaluating penny shares is a company's current earnings, probably one of the most important of the fundamental considerations in security analysis. Ask yourself, "Is the latest earnings positive compared to the same period a year ago?" If the answer is yes, then this makes for a buy candidate. Observes Bowser: "The very reason for a corporation's existence is to make a profit. Current earnings can indicate future prospects [and] the price of the company's stock reflects current earnings."

Ranking just behind earnings in importance is current sales (i.e., a company's sales during the ficsal year in progress). As Bowser points out, a decrease in sales may indicate that the company's products or services are not being well received. However, the decrease may also be due to economic conditions over which the firm has no control. "Nevertheless," he writes, "a decrease in sales is not a healthy situation, as we are looking for growth in both sales and earnings."

Clif Droke is the editor of the Junior Mining Stock Report and Gold Strategies Review newsletters. He is also the author of numerous books on financial market analysis. For more information visit www.ClifDroke.com

15

It's All About The People: What to Look for in a Company's Management Team

Dr. Richard S. Appel

My entrance into the gold stock arena was via the purchase of East Rand Proprietary Mines in 1972. This was a marginal South African gold producer who began production during the 1890s. They were slated to go out of business within a few years if the gold price did not raise from its then $50 an ounce price. At that time, and for the ensuing three decades, I invested in an untold number of gold and other primarily exploration companies. I was solely focusing upon the major projects that each company was pursuing.

I first entered the Canadian junior market in 1993. This was when gold's final, major, upward correction began, within its 20+ bear market. I had not yet altered my approach towards divining the next great profitable stock investment, and continued to search for the best "story" that I could find. However, to my detriment, many of the "stories" that were presented to me and that I believed, were essentially those conjured up by the minds of one various promoter or another.

When the Bre–X scandal exploded onto the exploration sector landscape in 1996, it hammered the final nail into the coffin of the junior companies for the next several years. From that point forward, until 2001, the junior companies basically withered away in price. I remained a distant observer until that year licking my earlier wounds, and wondering why my supposed great companies had gone bad. I thought that despite the market reversal, some of what I thought were exceptional companies surely should have succeeded.

After much soul-searching and questioning, it became evident to me that I had approached this volatile, yet incredible opportunity-wrought market, seeking the wrong company attributes. Rather than focusing on what appeared to be reasonably-priced companies with good projects, it dawned on me that a great project that is run by less than the best management team, is likely destined for failure. How could that be? That is the question that even I would never have asked several years earlier!

The reason is simple and obvious. Yet, it requires experience to fully understand and appreciate it. Until you invest in this industry for several years, and have suffered the consequences of believing that the project is all that is important, few would have a clue. It is the people that direct the companies that typically make the difference between possible success or failure.

The single most important factor that can make or break even the best company is its ability to raise working capital. Money is the lifeblood of any enterprise! And because the mining industry is so capital intensive, if a company runs out of money it has virtually no ability to advance its projects, let alone its share price. The next item that is essential to a junior company's future is its ability to acquire a substantial project. It is a given that their management is significantly talented to know how to make the most of each project. Finally, if the marketplace is not made aware of the value that a company's management has added to it, through a market awareness or promotional campaign, even an organization progressing a great project may see its stock languish for years. It is mandatory for all of these components to be in place for a company's shares to perform at their maximum level. This, in order to bestow upon their investors and management are profits that they have worked for and deserve.

The element that is missing from all but the few, very best junior resource companies is a group of directors that possesses all of these attributes. Some companies have exceptional promotional teams, but have little if any real projects of substance. Their shares will perform well for a while, until their insiders have taken their profits at the expense of their shareholders. A few experienced stockholders will ride the crest of these company's public relations campaigns. If they're nimble, they will sell their stock at a profit. Unfortunately, most investors that are attracted to the "story" as it is told, and buy at or near the top of the stock's run, will likely retain their stockholding until most of their original investment has dwindled away.

Other companies have the ability to attract money because their investors have profited from following their directors in other associated fields. Unfortunately, if a management team was successful in discovering a natural gas, oil or nickel deposit, it doesn't mean that they have the ability to find a gold or silver mine. A different type of expertise is needed for each of these endeavors. However, with the money that they are capable of raising, those boasting earlier successes will at least have an opportunity to attract one or more important projects as well as exceptional staff members. Remember, major companies or individuals who control the best projects will seldom vend them to a company unless they feel that their future partner can finance and properly manage the needed exploration. The vendor will only seriously profit through a discovery or hopefully when a mine is brought into production.

Still other companies are able to attract world class projects due to their prior success in bringing one or more mines into existence. Further, these management teams normally have little difficulty attracting capital because they have a history of making money for their stockholders. However, for one reason or another they often lack either the desire or the ability to bring sufficient market attention to their companies. This prevents them from moving their share prices to the sufficiently high levels that they deserve. They do have the best likelihood for ultimate success. Yet, they are forced to issue too many shares at low prices, in their effort to acquire sufficient working capital to advance their projects. This causes them to shortchange themselves and their stockholders, even in the event that they make yet another economic mine.

To my mind, the ideal companies of which there are a paltry few, are directed by a management team that has one or more important discoveries under their belt. For self-serving reasons, major mining companies and individuals within the industry recognize their ability, and desire to have them manage the exploration of some of their main projects. In this fashion the vendors have the best opportunity to maximize the value of the projects they possess, without incurring substantial financial expenditures unless success is at hand. For this reason these successful junior managers are regularly offered the best available projects from which they can pick and choose. Also, due to the fact that they have a long list of investors that have profited from their earlier relationships with them, they have little difficulty in attracting virtually any quantity of money that may be required. Finally, they recognize the importance of making the market aware of their acquisitions, progress and developments; in order to boost its share price to a level commensurate with their company's worth. Lesser management teams on the other hand, seldom have the opportunity to acquire anything other than reworked or secondary projects that have far less opportunity for exploration success.

Now to the real world, most of best-managed junior companies possess many, but not all, of these qualities. The one that is most often lacked is the desire or effort to bring the attention of the marketplace to their stock. Many of these extremely successful and talented individuals believe that their ultimate success will cause investors to clamor for their shares. While they are correct, this has both positive and negative implications for the investor. First, their share price will typically lag behind its deserved market value until they have sufficiently progressed their project, and it stands out from others in the industry. On a positive note, this gives the patient investor the ability to carefully follow their progress and increase their stockholdings at the most opportune times. In this fashion they can ride the crest of their management's success and still cheaply acquire their last shares.

I believe that it is incumbent upon anyone who invests in the resource sector to regularly keep in touch with their companies. It is best to develop a relationship with someone in their management rather than in their public relations staff. With practice you will learn to ask the right questions in order to ascertain whether your company has the right qualities that are necessary to give them at least an above average opportunity for success. You truly owe it to yourself to make your best effort to pick the most likely teams for success. Learning how to operate in this industry, as in all other aspects of life, is an ongoing process. You will certainly make mistakes. We all do!

I continue to err in judgment myself. However, they are becoming fewer and further in between. Don't berate yourself, but try to learn from your mistakes. I do my best to feature companies in Financial Insights that are relatively new in their development and that I believe offer exceptional relative value. In this fashion anyone investing in them should reduce their downside risk. For success in this market it is best to avoid stocks that appear overvalued when compared with their peers. If they seem overpriced, they likely are. Remember, the higher a stock's price the further it can fall.

Richard Appel publishes commentary on gold, the financial markets, as well as various junior resource stocks that offer great price appreciation potential. He is also in the process of beginning a hedge fund that will specialize in the junior natural resource sector. For more information visit www.FinancialInsights.org.

16

Uranium Stocks: An Interview with Kevin Bambrough, Market Strategist for Sprott Asset Management

Stock Interview: What do you look for in an exploration play before you even consider it?

Kevin Bambrough: There are different things you could do. With some exploration plays, you focus on management history. A lot of it is a belief in management. Sometimes you're looking at your belief in a region or the success of a region, which is called "closeology." Somebody's staked around an area where there was a recent strike by another. Or, a major dropped a bunch of land that was prospected around an existing deposit and another company picked up that land during a market low and is now going to explore.

Stock Interview: When you say a good management team, are you referring to the geological team?

Kevin Bambrough: Typically, yes. I get more comfort from guys that have worked for some of the larger companies. For example, some of them have been employed with a larger company for a long period of time in a prominent role. Then, they decide to go on their own because they feel that they can. They're excited to go and try to develop their own company. They think that they can go and hopefully strike it rich.

Stock Interview: Aren't there, however, a lot of failures in that area?

Kevin Bambrough: A lot of successes, too. It's a risk-to-reward ratio.

Stock Interview: Because the last uranium boom was thirty years ago, aren't many of the exploration companies having a tough time finding talented experts?

Kevin Bambrough: There are not a lot of people out there. There are some people who have been trained. The Altius (TSX: ALS) people were fortunate enough to work with Cameco and have had access to their lab over the last decade and are very close in that area. A lot of different people out there have skills, and people are developing them. Some would argue there are still a lot of people that are going to retire over the coming years and this skilled labor could get somewhat worse. But at the same time, there's a lot of new interest moving into this sector.

Stock Interview: How do you uncover the "hidden value" of a company in which you consider investing?

Kevin Bambrough: When we first started to look at uranium companies at the start of this bull market, we looked at different things they had. With a company like Western Prospector (TSX: WNP), it had a mineshaft. An existing shaft costs huge dollars to build today. Their market cap was less than the value of the shaft when we first started investing in it. Another company might have a database with drill data they can use. They just have to drill a few holes to be able to qualify their resources and bring things forward. So, it's a huge considerable cost and time savings. When you have access to that data, it's a type of hidden value. Sometimes, there are companies that have a mill that can be rehabilitated. In comparing the value of an explorer, in terms of one who's got a very little bit of drilling done on their property, you find out what it costs for the average drill hole. Depending upon where you are, it can be quite expensive. That also helps put a baseline value in the company.

Stock Interview: What about exploring in a remote area, such as Namibia, where Paladin Resources (TSE: PDN) has had success?

Kevin Bambrough: It really depends upon your distance from infrastructure. In Namibia, there is a real shortage of water. It can be an extreme problem. It can be an extreme cost to get access to water that's required in the mining process. It doesn't kill the exploration, it just means you're going to have to find a lot more uranium in order to justify the capital costs. If you believe there's some uranium in this remote area, there better be a lot of uranium. That's because the cost to build a mine there is extreme. It's not like you can truck the ore out, because it's out in the middle of nowhere. So you're going to have to build a mine and a mill, and it becomes a lot more difficult. You also have to make sure there is a long enough reserve life so you can spread the capital cost of the infrastructure out over time.

Stock Interview: Do you still believe we can find strong price appreciation in the uranium sector?

Kevin Bambrough: Personally, I think there's a lot of speculation going on in the sector and some things maybe of lesser quality are . . . well, the access to capital seems quite easy right now in the sector. Some of these stocks have already had 30%–50%, like Paladin, on the year. It's a little staggering and obviously you get a little uncomfortable when things move up so fast. For certain stocks whose projects I believe are real, they can move forward, go into production and generate profits. We think they're going to do really well. At the same time, I'd caution people that investing in mining is difficult and is a risky business. For us, we get comfort in investing in more of the known projects where we consider the economics and justify the price we pay.

Stock Interview: You mentioned that "access to capital was easy right now in the sector"?

Kevin Bambrough: The money is just pouring into this sector with all of the financings. In some ways, it's good for the industry as a whole. It may not be the best thing for the uranium price long term, but the investments that have come in recent months are going to help find, or might find, new deposits and solve the [supply] deficit at some point. We're talking way off here, because it still takes a long time to find new deposits.

Stock Interview: Sprott Asset Management has invested heavily in the uranium exploration sector, and many have done well. Will you continue to support these companies?

Kevin Bambrough: What we have been doing is basically sticking with our winners and helping to finance them to take their project forward. We still believe we were fortunate enough that most of the projects we found and invested in early are the ones that are still the most likely to come on in the future. We feel we're backing the right horses, and we're going to sort of stick with that philosophy.

Stock Interview: How do you keep everything balanced in your funds with each of these investments?

Kevin Bambrough: We try to stay close to the stories that we follow. We always evaluate and try to make sure we can justify the prices. Sometimes, one stock may get ahead of itself relative to another, and we'll look to move money from one to another for a while. Maybe one of the plays catches up, and the other one has a setback, so we can move in. That's basically what we've been doing for the longest time now, mainly moving money around in the sector. Every now and then, some new prospective play comes along, or we see some drill results. Or something like Tournigan (TSX: TVC), which was a fairly recent new one that we got into. I believe that one (TVC) has great exploration potential so that is one that we're following. We're helping to fund them to do more exploration in the area.

Stock Interview: Many companies approach you with presentations to fund their exploration or development programs. What red flags show up that make you shy away from their projects?

Kevin Bambrough: There have been a number of presentations, where a lot of the uranium companies just come in right away and say, "We're in the Athabasca Basin or whatever and we hope to find . . . or, they don't really have anything to talk about in terms of why we should believe that their properties are that prospective. It makes me nervous when I see people that are very promotional like that. They just think that they're going to go and find one of these things. They just seem to be such optimists. I prefer to go with guys that are more conservative and say, "This is our plan." And, they seem to have a very well thought out plan of how they're going to try to find something. We want to see some drill holes with results that really give us some encouragement that there is something there. I'd rather get away from them trying to tell me about the history of the Athabasca Basin. Typically, we've shied away from investing in just pure land plays in the Athabasca Basin. It would be interesting to know— and I'm not aware of, how many conductors have been drilled in the Athabasca Basin that have found nothing. There has been a lot of exploration over there, over time. It's tough, it takes time, and it takes a lot of money. All these guys that have tried to find it and don't find anything? The stocks just get crushed, and they keep having to come back to get more money to drill more.

This interview is excerpted from <u>Investing in the Great Uranium Bull Market: A Practical Investor's Guide to Uranium Stocks</u>, by the Editors of Stock Interview. For more information please visit www.StockInterview.com.

17

Make Sure You Have Some Platinum Stocks in That Gold Portfolio

Kenneth J. Gerbino

Investors that understand the logic of owning gold and gold shares should also be aware of the platinum group metals, usually referred to as PGMs. The main components are platinum, palladium and rhodium. There are some more exotic molecular hybrids of the group as well, but they are of more interest to scientists than investors. I will focus on platinum in this chapter.

Platinum is actually more precious than gold and has developed a strong jewelry following to tag along with its position as the anti-smog metal since it is used in catalytic converters on cars and trucks. The bottom line from an investment standpoint is very simple. More people are coming into the modern 21st century because of world progress and technology. China and India automobile consumption and the normal global replacement of 700,000,000 motor vehicles in the next 15–20 years will use an awful lot of platinum.

Most of the platinum in the world is found in South Africa (75%) and most of the near surface, low cost and large, easy to mine deposits have been discovered a long time ago and the supply portion of the equation will now start to get very tight in the years to come. Demand has out stripped supply for the last six years by an average of 373 tonnes annually. That's $10 billion a year on average. These deficit numbers of the last two years have been much smaller, but I expect this could change as our 2.5 billion newly industrialized friends in India and China continue to expand even at modest rates with some recessions thrown in.

Platinum is mostly used for auto exhaust emission reduction, jewelry and various other industrial usages. Auto and industrial usage takes up about 54% of supply and jewelry takes up about 40%. Most importantly, as the world has to turn increasingly to diesel engines, platinum will become even more important as it cannot (so far) be commercially substituted by palladium in diesel engines for emission control. Although platinum is the rarest of the precious metals it is actually essential in the production of a wide range of goods from gasoline and paints to pacemakers, disk drives and anti-cancer drugs.

Over 75% of the platinum market is controlled by South Africa—a de facto monopoly. If one is looking for large amounts of platinum you have to go to South Africa. Almost 70% of the platinum in the world comes from an area in South Africa called the Bushveld. It is the geological structure of this area that spells out why platinum supply may not pick up very much in the future. Imagine a great bowl-like structure 295 kilometers across buried in the ground.

This is the Bushveld geological structure. Mother Nature coated the base of the bowl with a 1–2 meter thick platinum group metal rich rock substance. The edges of the bowl come close to surface and the platinum metals can be mined by accessing this outer area of the bowl from surface. But towards the middle of the bowl, 1,500–3,000 meters below the surface a lot of platinum could be found, but the cost of extracting it from such deep levels is extremely cost prohibitive. Because the "coating," or reef as it is called, is only at best 1–3 meters wide, it is a small area to extract the valuable rock. The fact that it is so narrow means all the mining must be done using a lot of manual labor. Bottom line: This deep area and the narrow mining widths will mean very high cost production and supply will be limited.

The next problem with supply is that because the South African Rand has appreciated so much in the last two years, the local price of platinum in rand terms is not high enough to justify the high capital costs to start production on several of the platinum projects in the country, which is bullish for the metal price. Also, the underground mining cost structure is now very high in rand terms. Therefore some projects may be cancelled and many are being delayed.

Because most of the world's platinum comes from South Africa it actually doesn't matter how high the rand goes. If it stays strong for years, then for a while, new platinum production will be curtailed from lack of investment, new supply will dwindle and the price will have to go up. Therefore platinum producers will benefit from the higher metal price, even though their costs will go up. This is a unique situation.

On the other hand, if gold mining becomes less and less profitable in South Africa due to the strong currency, then the S.A. gold mining industry may be in trouble because plenty of investment in gold mines outside of South Africa can still take place because there is gold elsewhere, and a supply of gold from other countries would still be available. The reality is that the currency risk for platinum companies that are producers, or who have low cost operations, is nullified because there is almost no where else to go. Hence, many of the same risks that apply to any other commodity do not apply to platinum. Supply of platinum may very well be constrained for many years. In the meantime, since global populations and middle class consumers are increasing daily, platinum demand will most likely be improving for decades. Since the metal is so rare and so useful, this looks to me like an excellent long-term investment opportunity. Also, the great hope on the horizon to replace gasoline engines in the future is fuel cells. And guess what? They rely on platinum.

With any commodity becoming very expensive industrial users find substitutes and then demand slows. But at $800–$1,300 an ounce this has not happened to platinum. And barring a major global recession, I expect platinum to remain in a high price range. Now even in the event of a global recession I would expect platinum to still remain above $550 an ounce. The reason is that during the last Asian meltdown (1996–1999) platinum demand actually increased from 4.9 million ounces to 5.6 million ounces. During the U.S. recession in 2001–2002, platinum demand increased from 5.6 million ounces to 6.2 million ounces. There are few goods or services that can claim what platinum did during those economic slowdowns.

If you are going to invest in platinum group metal companies (PGMs), make sure they have a higher grade deposit (over 5 grams per tonne), have more platinum than palladium and have ground on the outer rim of the Bushveld. Also, if they are already producers, the lower the cost structure, the better. Some of the usual suspects for platinum investments would be the following major producers, which trade as American Depository Receipts (ADRs are traded in the Pink Sheets market) in the U.S. Anglo Platinum (AGPPY), Impala Platinum (IMPUY) and Lonmin (LNMIY). We also own a small developmental platinum company called Eastern Platinum (ELR–Toronto).

The good news about platinum is that it is not a political metal and there is no overhanging supply in the hands of the printing press boys.

18

Why Small Market Capitalization Equals Large Gains

Jason Hommel

I no longer have time to research every stock tip that I get. I have to be motivated to even take a look. The things I look for are basic yet essential when shopping for any good deal. There are only two main questions. What is the price? And what do I get?

The price is the market capitalization, not the stock price. The market capitalization (or market cap) is the valuation of the company if you could buy all the shares at the current stock price. When you buy stock in a company with a $20 million dollar market cap, you are essentially saying, "Yes, this company should be worth $20 million dollars or more."

Here's another way to understand the market cap. If one company has a stock price of $2,000 per share, and only 1,000 shares issued, that's the same market cap as a $0.20 stock price with 10 million shares issued. Most people just don't understand that. So unless you know how many shares have been issued, you have no idea of the value of the company. The share price says absolutely nothing about whether a company is cheap or not, unless you know how many shares have been issued. Trying to buy a "penny stock" at a $0.11 share price says nothing about whether the company may be cheap or not, because they might have already issued 350+ million . . . or even billions of shares!

The figures to work with are the "outstanding" shares and the "fully diluted" shares. I usually consider fully diluted, which includes all warrants and options, because the only reason I'd buy a stock is for the bullish outlook, and under that assumption, I'd assume most or all warrants and options will be converted (and even more will be issued, as necessary). Shares "authorized" is something different. That is the total number of shares that the company could issue, without having a shareholder vote to increase the number.

To find out the number of shares fully diluted sometimes takes a little work. You can sometimes find a current number listed at a company's website, that's the fastest way, usually under "quick report," "share structure" or "company information." Or, you can look up the financial reports. Then you need to check the date of that number and scan the news releases from that date until today to see if any more shares have been issued through stock options or recent financings. Add up the numbers, then multiply by the share price, and that's the market cap.

Stock Price = SP
Fully Diluted Shares = FDS
Market Capitalization = MC

SP X FDS = MC

And remember to keep continuous track of the market cap as long as you own the stock. I recently saw one company issue $80 million worth of new shares at $0.50/share, which surely doubled the market cap, and removed a lot of the upside potential of the stock, because there's no way that they could spend that much on exploration in a single year. As a wise man said, "Anything the government can do, the private sector can do better"—referring to printing up excessive paper certificates.

I usually like to look at companies with market caps in the range of $50 to $100 million and under; usually, the lower the better. A true penny stock does not depend on the share price, but rather, the size of the market cap! But I don't just buy all companies with a tiny market cap, which can also be dangerous. Share price is also important. I don't like to buy stocks under $0.20/share. Many people in the U.S. pay 1 penny per share in commissions, and at $0.10, that's a 10% hit. This is rather steep, even steep at 5% on a 20-cent stock.

Excessively low share prices are an odd thing that has happened to the Canadian mining industry. A hundred years ago, the average stock price in the U.S. was about $100. Since the dollar was worth about 50 times more back then, that's about $5,000 share price equivalent. That's a stock price that would make sense because people would consider a single share as a real investment.

But the market tends to give people what they want, and stupid investors get what they deserve. Some investors who don't understand market cap and who just want a "cheap" share price have created an odd type of demand that the mining industry has served by creating company share structures that create stocks under $1/share.

But the irony is that this "serving the market demand for penny stocks" has two major drawbacks for the companies that have engaged in it. It has created two trade barriers. First, there is the 1 penny commission that many brokers charge, which amounts to a 10% commission on a 10-cent stock. Second, many American institutions have charters that prevent them from buying stocks that are priced under $5/share.

Canadian companies would do themselves a big service if they did reverse splits to get their share prices into the $5–10 range. And furthermore, many brokers at major brokerage houses in the U.S. are forbidden from even recommending stocks priced under $5/share. The exploration industry may complain about lack of analyst coverage, but many analysts cannot cover the stocks. But I shouldn't complain. Wall Street's failure to cover the sector has given me an enormous advantage and allowed me to profit from my newsletter.

Next, it depends on what they have. A one to five million dollar market cap might be pricey if they don't have a great land package. I like to buy leverage. I want the most for my money.

Therefore, I look for superlatives. The highest grades. The biggest projects. The best location.

I do not like to buy unknown exploration potential. I like to buy freshly drilled resources that are higher grades and bigger projects than the market seems to realize and recognize. Not all potential projects will ever get funded to production. Many of the projects in the natural resources sector are 30 years old, or older! Some of these are now becoming potential winners. The projects that will be the most likely to attract major funding are those that tend to be the biggest, with the highest grades.

I tend to stay away from the smaller projects, with marginal grades, that will require $50 to $100 million to be put into production. I also like to stay focused on location; primarily within North America. Latin America is turning increasingly towards confiscating mining projects again. I've seen problems with Honduras, Bolivia, and Peru in just the last 3 years. Remember that about 70% of the world's oil is being produced by national governments who have confiscated the discoveries. This is why less oil discoveries are being made, in my opinion, due to world communism/confiscation.

The money moves into this sector in big waves. As it leaves, and stock prices drop, the sector seems to get sleepy and people stop paying attention to the news releases. This is the time to stay awake and do a lot of research, and see which projects are moving forward the fastest.

Some people say that this is a people business. I don't know about that. When I buy silver, I'm doing that because I think most people are fools who foolishly hold too much fraudulent paper money and bonds, overvalued houses, and overvalued stocks. I'm not betting on people being wise, I'm betting that they are foolish, because so few own silver.

Most mining company explorers do not own silver. That's already one major strike against them, showing how foolish they already are. Furthermore, no miners are even attempting to use silver as money, as a company; as a place to put company funds, and to offer to pay employees in silver. How utterly foolish.

Again, strike two. If I had to bet on people, I wouldn't bet on most of them!

I think this is a numbers business. A good track record means little to me. I reason, just because you have discovered something in the past, is no guarantee that you know what's under the ground in the next area. Furthermore, if an explorer has a great track record, then he's probably got plenty of investors ready to follow his moves and bid up the stocks excessively. I'd almost rather invest with a man who does not have a great track record, has difficulty finding funding, and has problems promoting his company. Because those things can be fixed, and you can hire people to take care of that if the project is good and worthy. The best people (explorers and developers) and money will gravitate to the best projects—as I've seen time and time again. And sometimes, the money gets there first, and that's what I try to do. Otherwise, you are a follower. And the later you get there, the more you pay. That's the way it works in this "first come, first served" world we live in.

Ideally then, I like a small market cap company, with plenty of drilled up resources located in North America, run by guys who are poor promoters. That sounds like two of my top three stocks for 2006, which rose about 200% & 400% this year alone. The third, which was up 600% had the smallest market cap and does not have drilled up resources yet. We're awaiting drill results now. I hope the results come back positive, and I hope investors stay awake.

Jason Hommel is the owner/editor of The Silver Stock Report. He writes a weekly column highlighting the gold, silver, money, and precious metals markets, including silver and gold stocks. Visit www.SilverStockReport.com and sign up for your free 'Silver Stock Report Newsletter' today.

19

Warrants: What They Are and How to Profit With Them

Dudley Pierce Baker

Readers of this book are obviously interested in the bull market in precious metals and have a genuine interest in junior mining stocks as do we. Our personal investment views are to capitalize to the maximum on this bull market by allocating some investment capital (10%–20%) to long-term warrants on some of our favorite mining companies. We have come to realize that many in the investment community, including many professionals, do not fully understand warrants. So allow us to explain the benefits of warrants and their place in your investment portfolio.

THE MOST OVERLOOKED INVESTMENT VEHICLE TODAY

Most investors are familiar with options on stocks—calls and puts, right? I, like many of you, realize this is a very dangerous game for most investors. An option gives you the right, not the obligation, to acquire the underlying security/stock at a specific price and expires at a specific date in the future. However, options are very short term, usually 30, 90 or 180 days, so you have to be not only correct with respect to your timing but also with respect to the direction of the stock market. Perhaps you are a better market timer than most, but options do not work out well for most investors.

A warrant is very similar to a call option but with one major difference: Time! Warrants are usually issued with a minimum of 2 to 5 years of life. This means we as investors have the right to acquire the underlying stock at a specific price (determined by the company) and expiring at a specific date in the future. Warrants are usually issued by companies in connection with a financial arrangement and/or public offering and are a "kicker" to sweeten the deal. As investors in warrants, our objective is to only trade the warrants with no intention of ever exercising them.

Currently there are many warrants trading with expiration dates out to the year 2011, and perhaps even longer, depending on when you read this book. Warrants expiring within, say, 2 years, while they may possess great upside leverage, also pose a greater risk. Thus, it is widely recommended for most investors to focus on warrants with at least 2 years left before expiration, giving you more time to play this bull market cycle.

Can you imagine having the right, but not the obligation, to purchase the common shares of one of your favorite mining or energy companies with up to 5 years before expiration? Of course warrants, like options, do not come without some risk. If the underlying stock is trading below exercise price on the expiration date, the warrant will expire worthless. This is why we strongly recommend investors focus on warrants that have a remaining life of at least 2 years.

WHY YOU SHOULD BE INTERESTED IN WARRANTS

I've had the opportunity to visit at length with two of the most savvy and respected professionals in the business, Frank Holmes and Martin Weiss. Both agree that warrants have a place in an investor's portfolio. This fact alone should peak your interest.

Warrants are all about leverage. Leverage is why all investors should consider warrants. If your favorite mining stock has a warrant trading you should take a serious look to see if it fits your investment criteria (i.e., how long does the warrant have until expiration and does it provide good leverage?). It is not always easy to find all the facts on the warrants for some companies. You should always do your homework, unless you allow us to do it for you in our service.

What does leverage mean? Leverage means getting the maximum return with the least amount of your investment capital at risk. Most investors are looking for at least a 2:1 ratio; in other words, if the common stock doubles (i.e. 100%); we are looking for a minimum 200% move in the price of the warrant. Perhaps the best way to explain 'leverage' is by the example in the next paragraph.

In 2006, the top performing warrant in our database was Blue Pearl Mining (TSX: BLE) with a return of 3,729%. The common stock was up 1,310% and thus the warrant outperformed the common stock by 2.85:1. The warrant of Blue Pearl Mining gives the holder the right, but not the obligation, to acquire the common stock at a price of CDN$0.70 at or before the expiry date of 22 March 2007. So, had you been interested in Blue Pearl Mining at the end of 2005, we would have asked the question: Why not buy the warrants? We make our decisions based on the leverage factor and remaining life of the warrant.

Blue Pearl Mining	Dec 2005	Dec 2006	ROI
Common Stock	C$0.70	C$9.87	1,310%
Warrant	C$.24	C$9.19	3,729%
Leverage			2.85:1

(For each $1,000 invested in the warrants of Blue Pearl Mining you could have made $37,290)

PRECIOUS METALS WARRANTS INDEX

One more reason to be excited about including warrants in one's portfolio is evidenced by the Precious Metals Warrants Index (PMWI). The Precious Metals Warrants Index is our own proprietary index and includes all warrants outstanding for 12 months as of year-end. In 2005, the index increased 51.4% and in 2006 the index was up an unbelievable 183.5%! This by far exceeds even our expectations. Here is a list of other prominent precious metals indices and their performance in 2006 compared to the PMWI:

INDICES	2006
PMWI (Precious Metals Warrant Index)	183.5%
GoldColony.com (Index of Junior Gold Stocks)	55.5%
USERX (U.S. Global Investors Gold Shares)	50.2%
Silver	45.5%
Gold	23.0%
UNWPX (U.S. Global Investors–World Precious Minerals Fund)	34.2%
HUI (Amex Gold Bugs Index)	22.0%
Dow Jones Industrial Average	16.3%
S&P 500	13.6%
XAU (PHLX Gold & Silver Sector Index)	11.0%

Footnote: The Precious Metals Warrants Index is a Price Weighted Index and includes all warrants, which were trading for at least 12 months.

BROKERAGE FIRMS

We believe that virtually all of the brokerage firms will execute the trades in the warrants. However, you may find you need to educate your broker. The commissions may vary greatly from firm to firm, so we suggest you verify the commissions before you place your orders. If you find your current broker will not cooperate with you on placing orders for warrants, or perhaps their commissions are very high, we suggest you contact www.NetVest.com. We have used this discount broker for over 20 years and their maximum commission on warrants is $29, whether you buy 100 or 100,000. We have no financial interest in this company other than being a satisfied customer for many years.

United States investors: Virtually all of the warrants trading are on Canadian companies. Currently 50% of these warrants have U.S. symbols and thus your orders can be placed using your online broker. For the other warrants, it will be necessary to call your broker to place these orders. The broker will usually have to call his back office/clearing firm to get the correct symbol for placing the order. The most important thing to do first is give your broker the CUSIP number for the warrant you wish to purchase.

Canadian investors: As there are symbols for all the Canadian warrants, your placing of orders should be very easy and we would think you can use your online brokerage firm as the symbols are clearly established for these warrants.

Dudley Pierce Baker is the owner/editor of Precious Metals Warrants, a market data service that provides subscribers with up to date news and information on mining and energy companies that have warrants trading in the United States and Canada. For more information please visit www.PreciousMetalsWarrants.com.

20

Quantifying Silver Stocks' Leverage

Roland Watson

What is the main reason investors buy silver mining stocks? Is it because they like a bit of geopolitical risk or is it because the next set of drill tests may or may not produce the expected big find? No, the answer is summed up in one word—leverage. To put that in plain numbers, if silver goes up by 10% over a given period but a given silver stock goes up by 30%, then the leverage that stock gives over silver is bullish at 3 (i.e. 30 divided by 10). However, if they both go up by 20% then the stock is deemed to have offered zero leverage against silver at a neutral value of 1.

That may seem like a great return, but why own a stock with all its associated risks when solid and safe silver is offering the same rate of return? You don't, and the stock leaves your portfolio. Worse still, if our silver company made only a small gain of 10% while silver powered on by 20% then our anemic stock is offering a bearish leverage of 0.5. Sayonara, hapless stock!

But what we need is a means to quantify leverage and that is what we plan to show you here. First note that leverage (or gearing) is a delta function. In other words, it measures two different points. It doesn't do snapshots at one time, but differences over time. At this point we introduce our volunteer stock, and a well favored one at the time of writing, ECU Mining Inc. Here is a recent closing price chart.

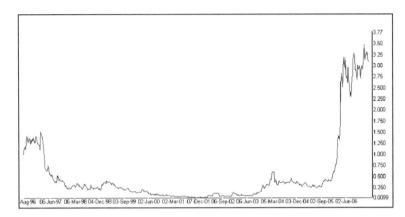

I envy the one who boarded this stock at 25 cents for they have fully taken advantage of a seriously leveraged stock. Now, if we mimic the advice of the mutual fund managers who suggest that stocks should be held for at least several years before cashing out, what do we get if we calculate a leverage period of four years? And how do we produce the corresponding leverage chart?

Using the first point on the graph to explain the charting method, we divide the closing price of ECU on the 7th August 2000 ($0.09) by the closing price of ECU four years previously on the 6th August 1996 ($0.95). We repeat this procedure for silver. That gives us 0.095 and 0.972 respectively. Dividing the stock number by the silver gives us an ECU to silver leverage of 0.098. In other words, it stinks.

Between the 6th August 1996 and 7th August 2000, ECU Mining under performed silver by a factor of nearly 10 to 1! Needless to say, silver was in a bear market, but poor ECU was in the cage with the bear! Now what happens if we start rolling through the subsequent years to the present day? By "rolling" I mean we roll on one day and repeat the four-year calculation for the next two sets of days (7th August 1996 and 8th August 2000) and so on until the present day. Bring all these data points together and you have the graph below.

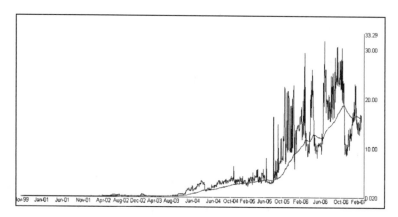

Now we have a bull trend we can talk about! From a meager leverage of less that 0.02 in the dark days of 2001, ECU boarded a rocket as it hit the heights of outperforming silver by over 30 to 1 in 2006! Remember that leverage greater than 1 means the stock is outperforming silver on a four-year basis. When did that happen on this chart? To make things clearer we convert to a semi-log scale below and superimpose the ECU share price.

I have annotated a couple of things here. The line at which the ECU leverage hits 1.00 is shown as the horizontal line. On the 24th December 2003, it broke decisively above this line to become an outperformer and never looked back. Looks like Santa Claus had come a day early for serious silver stock investors. Anyone getting on at this leverage signal was onto a literal ten-bagger.

When one sees such huge gearings on the price of silver, they are inevitably down to one thing. The company in question has seen significant reserve growth via discovery. Meaning, they have finally hit pay dirt with a big find or their current deposits have been substantially upgraded. Not surprisingly, in that 33 to 1 leverage timeframe, ECU went from 25 cents a share to over 3 dollars a share.

This is because companies such as ECU will leverage two quantities. They leverage the price of silver but also the amount of silver under their control. Once investors have assimilated this new reserves information and adjusted the share price accordingly, the leverage goes back to purely leveraging the market price of silver.

Now the ECU leverage has dropped from about 30 down to 10 and back up to 15. We do not expect to see such leverage numbers again from ECU unless another big discovery turns up. And even then leverage will proceed more sluggishly as it is more difficult for a stock to double from $3 to $6 than it is for it to double from $ 0.25 to $0.50. Nevertheless, if the leverage were to keep dropping, an exit strategy should be in place. One could suggest a return to a leverage of 1 as an exit point, but by then the price may have dropped too much. It is wise to consider other indicators in conjunction with the leverage indicator to time an exit for this stock. But that is another story for another time.

Finally, I may note that this four year rolling leverage chart is not the same as a chart produced by dividing the price of the equity by the price of silver. One must know that a stock's performance is calculated by comparing two prices over a certain time period. Dividing the silver and ECU prices from the same day does not measure leverage although it can show in a qualitative manner that it is outperforming or underperforming silver.

By using a leverage chart such as the one examined here, the performance question can be quantified by the simple fact that if the leverage drops below 1 it is underperforming silver and if it goes above 1 it is outperforming silver. A simple stock to silver price ratio cannot convey this information. We recommend this technique as part of your stock picking strategy.

Roland Watson writes "The Silver Analyst," an investment newsletter dedicated to silver and only silver. He has been writing precious metals investment and economic articles for various websites since 2001 and first invested in precious metals in 1997. For more information please visit www.SilverAnalyst.blogspot.com.

21

10 Types of Deposits and the Cash Minerals Locked Inside Them

Kevin Corcoran

Knowledge is power. And in the junior mining and exploration sector, the more you know about different minerals, grades and deposits, the better chance you have in correctly identifying the next "10-bagger". The resource stock investor should learn about the various types of mineral deposits. Different deposits require certain grades or tonnage to be economically feasible at the current market price of the underlying commodity.

For instance, porphyry-style deposits that contain copper are typically "low" grade and require relatively larger tonnage than volcanic massive sulphide deposits. Placer deposits are usually mined at surface and since the minerals are hosted in "loose" sediment, they have the potential to be mined at low cost. Here is a list of the different types of deposits and the minerals commonly found in them:

Placer deposits are an accumulation of sand and gravel in modern or ancient streambeds containing valuable minerals including gold, platinum (PGMs), tin, and titanium. Placer deposits are typically surface deposits found within sedimentary rocks and can be billions of years old, such as the Witwatersrand deposits in South Africa.

Epithermal deposits are formed when volcanic activity pushes magma through vents forming high-grade vein systems with low-grade bulk tonnage found at shallow depths in regional fault systems. Minerals present include gold, silver, zinc, lead, copper, molybdenum, and manganese. Examples include Barrick's Pierina mine in Peru and Goldcorp's El Sauzal mine in Mexico.

Volcanic-Hosted Massive Sulphides (VMS) are a type of metal sulfide ore deposit, mainly copper-zinc, that are associated with and created by volcanic hydrothermal events. The mineralogy of VMS deposits consists of over 90% iron sulfide. As a class, VMS deposits represent a significant source of the world's copper, zinc, lead, selenium, cadmium, tin, gold, and silver. The majority of world deposits are small, with about 80% of known deposits in the 0.1–10 million tonne range. Examples of VMS deposits are Kidd Creek, Ontario, Canada; Brunswick #12, New Brunswick, Canada; Las Cruces (Rio Tinto), Spain.

Skarns are the world's premier sources of tungsten. They are also an important host of copper, iron, molybdenum, zinc, gold, tin, and other metals. Skarns also serve as sources of industrial minerals such as graphite, asbestos, and magnesite.

Porphyry deposits are formed when a column of rising magma is cooled in two stages. In the first stage, magma is cooled slowly deep in the crust, creating large crystal grains with a diameter of 2 mm or more. In the second stage, magma is cooled rapidly at a relatively shallow depth or as it erupts from a volcano, creating small grains that are usually invisible to the unaided eye. The cooling also leads to a separation of dissolved metals into distinct zones. This process is one of the main reasons for the existence of rich, localized metal ore deposits such as those of gold, copper, molybdenum, lead, tin, zinc, and tungsten. The ore bodies typically contain between 0.4 and 1% copper but can be higher.

Iron-Oxide-Copper-Gold (IOCG) deposits have large concentrations of low-titanium, iron oxide minerals, mainly magnetite and hematite, as opposed to iron sulphides typical of porphyry copper-gold systems. IOCGs host copper, uranium and gold, as well as numerous other lesser-known metals. Examples of IOCG deposits are Carajas, Brazil; Palabora, South Africa; and BHP Billiton's Olympic Dam deposit in southern Australia.

Mesothermal Veins: Mesothermal gold deposits are formed from hot water that precipitates gold under high temperatures and pressure, generally at great depths in the earth's crust (around 10km). In these deposits, high gold grades tend to be continuous over large vertical ranges. This process has formed throughout geologic history but younger examples include the Mother Lode District in California and the Bralorne-Pioneer District in British Columbia. Nearly 80% of B.C.'s gold production has been mined from mesothermal veins, including Almaden's Elk Gold Mine.

Greisen deposits are significant sources of tin, tungsten, or molybdenum. The term greissen in German means "to split," and was used in reference to coarse-grained aggregates of quartz and muscovite found on the borders of tin veins in granites. Greisens host some of the world's most important tin deposits including those in Tasmania, Australia; the Bolivian Tin Belt in the Andes; and Cornwall-Devon in southwest England. Also, many of the tungsten deposits in southeast China, the richest tungsten province in the world, are found in greisenized granite. Gold and silver are mined in greisen deposits as byproducts.

Nickel Massive Sulphide deposits host nickel, copper and platinum group metals. Ore bodies such as the Voisey's Bay deposit consist mainly of sulphide minerals in which nickel, copper and cobalt are chemically bound to sulphur.

Kimberlites: Diamonds are the most significant mineral extracted from kimberlite. They occur in regions of thick and stable continental crust, in southern Africa (including the Kimberley district), India, Siberia, Canada, Colorado-Wyoming, Venezuela, and Brazil. Most kimberlite outcrops appear on the surface as small, roughly circular areas less than 1 km (0.6 mi) in diameter. They are usually not well exposed because kimberlite weathers rapidly. In three dimensions, kimberlite bodies are dikes, or more commonly, downward-tapering cylinders. Chromium is also found in kimberlite pipes in economical grades.

22

How to Profit on the Road to Failure

Dr. Richard S. Appel

I believe the following can help prepare the reader to success-fully navigate this potentially highly profitable area by better understanding how the mining industry works. This includes both the positive conditions and attributes that a company must possess in order to succeed, as well as the various obstacles that must be avoided when one speculates in this exciting stock segment. Given my belief that the junior mineral exploration sector is on the cusp of a major advance, I feel that sharing my thoughts at this time is quite timely. I hope the following will help both the novice and expert investor approach these stocks in a different light, and will give all readers a better perspective of what to look for and what to avoid, whenever they evaluate a potential investment in this area.

It is my desire as the reader peruses this missive that they will benefit from my intent. I hope you recognize that substantial profits can be acquired without owning a company that either makes a major mine or is taken over by another enterprise. If the truth were known, most of those who have amassed the greatest fortunes speculating in this market have done so by putting to use what I now recognize and describe below.

One issue that is rarely mentioned in the junior exploration industry is the fact that few companies actually bring a mine into production. Some are successful in taking a discovery to the feasibility stage. Yet, rarely does a mineral deposit, let alone a substantial one, actually generate cash flow or a profit to the company. This truth should always be kept in mind whenever one evaluates a junior resource stock. But also never lose sight of the reality that it is not necessary for a mining company to ever turn a profit, in order for the knowledgeable, astute investor to garner substantial capital gains.

A few years ago a very capable and successful geologist confided in me some very unusual and, at the time, very upsetting information. He worked a number of years for a major, profitable mining company, Cominco Ltd. The company operated in numerous countries and had decades of mineral exploration and mining experience. Cominco was since acquired by Teck Corporation, and the surviving entity is now Teck Cominco Ltd.

I believe that it was during the early 1990s, when one of their directors desired to compare their successes with their failures. To this end, he ordered an evaluation of all projects in which Cominco expended $1 million or more for exploration. For newcomers to the mineral exploration business a large number of potential mineral targets are eliminated before the $250,000 level of expenditures is reached. The fact that a major company continues to work on a property and incurs over $1 million of expenses indicates their great belief in the likelihood of the project's becoming a mine.

Industry wide, after $1 million dollars is spent, very few projects remain which a company believes warrant further exploration. These are indeed the best of the best. Unfortunately, of these, few actually become mines. Invariably, what appeared to be highly prospective ground fails to meet the necessary criteria for the company to continue working on it.

In the case of the Cominco study, their researchers found over 2,000 projects upon which over $1 million was expended. From this pool, the company only made six or seven mines. Think about that for a moment! This gives you an idea of the actual likelihood of a junior company developing a project to the point where it is either bought out by a major company, or proceeds into production. However, it also gives one insight into the enormous profits that can be garnered if an investor picks one of the few companies that will reach the ultimate goal of mining success. After all, Cominco began as a small concern and grew to generate substantial profits during its decades long existence, and greatly rewarded its shareholders in the process. The rewards that Cominco and other major mining companies bestow upon their shareholders is enormously magnified if a junior miner is successful. In this instance, a company worth pennies can see its shares skyrocket in price, and move into the multi-dollar range.

The reason I'm presenting this information is not to frighten investors about the junior exploration market. It is to help you better understand the industry and to make you aware that given all of the potential difficulties and pitfalls that must be dealt with, there are ways in which savvy investors can be quite successful and continually garner substantial profits.

I am in the forefront of those who desire to pick companies that have the qualities necessary to move a project to a profitable conclusion. I still believe! Fortunately, I have been able to early recognize a number of companies that grew from the exploration stage to be either acquired by a major corporation, or moved into production. When this occurred, I was not only compensated for losses that I sustained from a number of companies that were not so fortunate, but I was left with an impressive, overall profit. Finding a company that generates such success should be viewed as the icing on the cake! If an investor can control a normal amount of greed which we all possess, he can not only position himself for a great wind-fall, that a truly successful junior company can generate, but he can also profit from companies that are fated for failure.

The primary necessary ingredient for success in the junior exploration industry is the people! I will assume that those managing any company in which you choose to invest are responsible for at minimum a major discovery or have actually been instrumental in building one or more mines. This immediately eliminates the vast number of junior mining companies! Further, they must also be capable of acquiring capital with which to carry out their exploration programs, and must have the ability to successfully present their story to the investment community. Additionally, it is typically best to enter such a company's stock while it is quietly developing its projects rather than when it is in the midst of a surging share price created by some element of successful progress.

During all bull markets, whether of an entire market or an individual stock, there are always secondary, downward corrections. It is during these periods, such as I believe we are just exiting in the resource sector, when an astute investor can acquire fine companies at substantial discounts to their earlier highs. In this fashion you can have significant information about the company, while exposing yourself to less risk due to its reduced price level.

One of the qualities that I look for whenever I evaluate a company to feature in Financial Insights, is that it is in the early stages of its development. It may take a while, but if you have a proven management team these companies offer the best risk vs. reward potential in the industry. Further, they give their investors the greatest opportunity for exceptional profits. The time to acquire your share position is when a company's stock is quiet, its price is weak, and it is in the beginning stages of its development. The worst is when other investors are clamoring for it, and are driving up the price. You will learn that when everyone seems to want to purchase your shares, is the exact time when you should actually be doing some selling! With these conditions and concepts firmly understood and followed, one has the opportunity to benefit from the great volatility inherent in this market.

HOW CAN AN INVESTOR GARNER SUCCESS WHILE RECOGNIZING THAT HIS COMPANY IS LIKELY DESTINED TO FAIL?

I believe this can be best explained by following a company through a typical cycle in the junior exploration sector. Whether a company begins its existence as an initial public offering or was dormant for a period due to an earlier failure, they all emerge by raising their initial working capital. This usually comes from members of their management team and from investors who are familiar with the directors, and who have confidence in their abilities.

The company then searches for what they believe is an attractive exploration target or advanced stage project. As an aside, the best projects usually find their way into the hands of those mining men who have met with past great success. Occasionally, what appears to be a dormant company, or shell, may announce an important acquisition. In this event, overnight, the company's value can enormously increase and its share price may soar.

After acquiring their initial project, the junior company prepares for their first exploration campaign. During each stage of exploration a company has the potential to meet with some form of success. For example, early geophysical or geochemical evaluations might be sufficient to allow the company to announce the discovery of a geological setting that is highly conducive to hosting an important mineral deposit. Or, as they proceed and begin to test the rock types through chip or channel samples, they may report high-grade results. As progress continues and if they advance to the drilling stage, the company might be fortunate to state that they "pulled a hole" that had a significant, if not spectacular mineralized intercept. In all of these events, it is likely the marketplace will become excited and investors may sharply bid up its share price.

The knowledgeable investor, who owned the stock before any of these milestones occurred, will utilize these price advancing periods not to add to his position, but to take some profits!

He will do this with the knowledge that the majority of the positive effect upon the share price will likely only be temporary, and he will use the occasion to recoup some or all of the initial capital that he invested in the company.

This is not to say that a price movement from say $0.75 C. to the $1.25 C. to $1.50 C. or higher range will retreat back to its lift-off price of $0.75 C. The excitement that excellent field results generate tends to temporarily drive a company's share price further than is justified. This is normal price action. When the enthusiasm dissipates the stock will retreat to a better price indication of the company's new found value. If the news was truly important to the company, $0.75 C. may never be seen again.

Such times present the investor with not only the opportunity to reduce his financial exposure, but it also gives him the good fortune to own some promising stock, that has already increased in value, for little or nothing. The goal of successful investors in this industry is to possess a stock position that can be carried for as close to a zero cost basis as possible! Occasionally, if he is convinced that the success is not a flash in the pan, he will wait for the stock to pull back before adding to his position. However, he will do this with great care.

You must recognize that it is for a plethora of reasons why so few mines are actually built. It can be due to either acts of nature, the fallibility or overzealousness of man, a drop in the market price for the mined metal, or for an unending array of other reasons. For example, nature has a way of creating a very rich body of mineralization, but later, due to either erosion or one or a series of earth movements, it can either reduce its size or transport a portion of the deposit miles from where it was formed. Thus, initial encouraging surface geophysical or sampling results may have occurred because the remnants of an ore body may have been carried by an ancient river and were deposited at the site. When the company either performs channel sampling or drills the target, the ground beneath it might be barren of mineralization. Similarly, if a company discovers either a seemingly strongly mineralized open pit deposit or a very rich vein, they may later abandon the prospect because either the grade is insufficient, its tonnage is inadequate, the mineralized structure may be at too great a depth to economically mine, the project is too remote to infrastructure, the metallurgy is too complex, or the vein might pinch off or disappear. In each instance what initially appeared to be an exciting discovery may turn into a disappointment!

As for man, mistakes are made or a company's management may attempt a feat for which they are not sufficiently experienced. A great exploration geologist normally is unprepared to build a profitable mine. He may have the capacity to sense the presence of a great body of mineralization, but once the deposit is defined he should hand the mine's development to those who specialize in that field. Too often, a team of explorers will attempt to bring their discovery into production and fail.

Another reason for failure could occur during the feasibility stage if the costs are underestimated—they begin building the mine only to run out of capital for its completion. These are some of the reasons why even many impressive exploration results and even positive feasibility studies ultimately lead to the abandonment of the projects!

Yet, even in these instances the knowledgeable investor can profit! This is because excitement will likely be generated by the announcements of each positive press release. This will give him the opportunity to take profits, and at times they may be exceptional! To me, it is a given that well-managed companies will periodically generate market excitement as the current bull market in precious and base metals unfolds. Further, even if they are not successful with their first project, the finest management teams will find new ones in their continual search for success! Therefore, as your company progresses, it is virtually assured that your ability to take some money off the table should present itself on more than one occasion. This assumes that you have entered your stocks during their early stages of evolvement, and have the patience to allow them to develop.

In Financial Insights, I try to feature companies that I believe have a major head start over their competitors, and are early in their life cycles. Their management is either already successful or they are competent and possess assets that I believe are greatly unrecognized, which renders them undervalued by the marketplace. I attempt to initiate stock purchases before most investors even know of the company's existence. This limits my downside risk while it exposes me to far greater profits. In effect, I feature and buy solid, little-known companies at low prices, and sell them when they excite the marketplace and investors clamor for them. You should attempt to do the same!

In order to achieve success, a primary investor goal should be to own shares in as many companies as possible, while having as little of his or her own money at risk in any individual junior. Further, patience is mandatory for an investor to profit from speculating in this field! Remember, it normally requires five to seven years from the time of a "discovery," to profitable ore extraction if a mine is built.

Additionally, exploration is often hampered by any of a number of problems or conditions. They can range from weather, licensing or other government interferences, infrastructure construction, environmental considerations, or various negotiations that can delay a project's advancement. Further, even with the best of exploration experts, it often takes time to find and acquire the right project. Also, it can easily require one or more years for the negotiations of an exciting acquisition to actually be consummated.

These are among the reasons why I attempt to acquire shares during a company's early stages, and that are managed by those individuals whom I have the greatest confidence and trust. It allows me to purchase stock for pennies that have the potential to soar to multi-dollars. I am prepared to wait patiently as it could take one, two or even three or more years before the right conditions present themselves. However, I will comfortably and confidently await the rewards knowing that I have aligned myself with the best management teams in the industry.

If one of your companies successfully proceeds to the point of performing either a pre-feasibility or feasibility study, other opportunities and problems will arise. If investors believe that the project is nearing a mining decision they will normally bid up its stock price in anticipation. This gives the wise investor yet another chance to either recoup the balance of his investment in the company, or to even take some profits. He does this with the knowledge that one of a number of potential problems still lurks in the shadows that may kill it!

This might be caused by a metallurgical difficulty that can greatly impact the mining cost. It could arise from political, environmental or native problems, or the cost of building the mine might be too prohibitive. This could be due to the absence of adequate infrastructure such as electrical power, water, or roads, which would make the mine uneconomic. Additionally, the economics of the project might be insufficient for other reasons. This might prevent their management from acquiring the capital necessary for the mine's construction. Also, the sector's market condition might be poor at the time. This would discourage potential investors from offering the needed development capital.

Potential problems still remain to be overcome. In the event that a company announces a positive feasibility study and prepares to finance and build a mine, they're still not out of the woods. However, a decision to proceed with building a mine will virtually assure another wave of investor interest and a surging share price. Again, this offers the aware investor an opportunity to greatly profit from his initial investment. In this event, his remaining shares should now be worth many multiples of their original cost.

Among the possible pitfalls for the company as they proceed to production, are that they may realize they have underestimated some of their costs. Further, they may become entrapped in a legal battle. This can arise for a number of reasons. Someone may claim that they hold title to the property or were somehow cheated by the company. Or the local inhabitants, environmentalists, or the overseeing government might interfere with the permitting process and delay or prevent the mine's construction. However, if you have properly retrieved your original investment in the company these problems will barely affect you. You will possess free stock in the company and can patiently wait until the problems are resolved.

As you can see, the junior exploration sector has more than its share of problems and pitfalls. However, if you accept this you will actually take your first major step towards success! You will not depend upon a company to go into production for you to profit! You will make your mind up to utilize the periods that are destined to occur, when a company generates excitement during a given stage of its development, to sell your cheaply acquired stock and generate exceedingly handsome rewards. This will not prevent you from substantially profiting if one of your companies is either taken over or goes into production.

I have delved deeply into the workings of this industry because I want to educate the reader about the possible dangers that a company may encounter on its journey towards either success or failure. You should not feel threatened by these problems! Instead, I hope that you will now view them from a different perspective as I do. I recognize that I will not own many companies that will ultimately make a mine, or that will be acquired by a major company. However, I am confident that I will possess a number of stocks that will sufficiently excite the marketplace to drive their shares to substantial levels. If you follow my lead, this will allow us to take advantage of these fleeting, exciting and profitable periods when our shares soar, to take profits.

From experience, I am convinced that if managed properly, speculating in this field gives one the potential to meet with great financial rewards. This can best be achieved if you buy companies early in their development that possess the finest management, and sell some of your stock each time they achieve success.

The surging precious and base metals prices of the last few years have allowed the junior Canadian exploration industry to acquire an enormous amount of working capital. The total has been staggering and is unrivaled in the history of the industry. This has allowed a number of the Canadian explorers to acquire and develop their best projects to the point where I believe some major discoveries if not mining decisions will be announced.

In Financial Insights, I am closely watching several small companies that I feel have the potential to meet with tremendous success. They will not all work. However, if only one in five companies does, the overall profits should be substantial. When the next major discovery, takeover, or mining decision is announced, it will generate a substantial amount of excitement that will vibrate throughout the industry. This will bring what will likely become an unprecedented amount of capital into this tiny stock sector. When this transpires, it will act to drive the majority of stocks to higher levels. In essence it will raise the value and therefore the prices of the companies that participate in the industry. Further, the bull market in not only the precious metals but also in the various base metals, will transform numerous here-to-fore uneconomic deposits into wildly profitable ones. Uneconomic deposits will become economically viable because the value of their mineral content will soar. This will greatly enhance the value of the companies benefiting from this event, and will bring additional excitement and investor interest to the other junior mineral exploration companies. And with it, higher prices for the majority of their shares.

23

The Critical Role Mining ETFs Play in Your Investment Success

Kevin Corcoran

Exchange Traded Funds (ETF) are designed to provide exposure to stock indices, sectors, bonds, currencies, and commodities through the stock market. ETFs trade like stocks and offer diversification similar to mutual funds, making them ideal investment vehicles for many investors. New ETFs are rolling out continuously and the mining and metals sector has an increasing amount of funds that offer trading opportunities in the natural resource sector. ETFs can also be used to analyze and select individual stocks within a market sector.

I use ETFs to gauge relative strength in a sector. Before I initiate a long term position in a gold (or any resource) stock, I like to see other gold stocks creating a base or moving higher. I also want mining stocks to display leverage and make stronger gains than gold bullion. I can do this by setting a chart that compares the performance of gold mining companies to gold. In www.StockCharts.com (or any charting software), type "GDX:GLD" in the search field. This compares the performance of the AMEX Gold Miners Index to the StreetTRACKS gold bullion ETF. If GDX is rising against GLD, then mining stocks are outperforming the market price of gold.

In May 2005, the gold miners began to climb steadily for a run that lasted close to a year.

However, since April 2006, the gold mining index has been in a correction. Until the above resistance line is broken, it would be safer to hold bullion. Or even better, park your capital until the next leg-up is confirmed.

The second chart shows a recent increase in volume as GDX moved slightly lower against GLD, meaning optimism is still being wringed out of the mining sector—a sign that weak hands are folding and mining stocks will have very few sellers left to drive prices lower. Charts indicating volume increases and decreases will help you gauge trend direction, strength and investor sentiment. Find the sector that is experiencing greater money inflows and initiate trades accordingly.

The ETFs listed below track gold bullion, physical silver, base metals, futures contracts, mining companies, and commodity indices. You can trade a basket of the world's top gold miners, monitor large-cap multinational steel companies, or invest in the performance of the Toronto Stock Exchange. ETFs designed to provide exposure to commodities and mining companies are dynamic tools to track and trade the markets.

Market Vectors TR Gold Miners (AMEX:GDX)
Tracks the performance of the Amex Gold Miners Index made up of 38 stocks. The fund mainly invests in the gold and silver mining industry.

SPDR S&P Metals & Mining ETF (AMEX:XME)
Objective is to replicate the performance of the S&P Metals & Mining Select Industry Index.

Market Vectors Steel Index Fund (AMEX:SLX)
Seeks to track the performance of steel companies as represented in the Amex Steel Index. The Index currently consists of 36 securities, representing a diversified blend of small-, mid- and large capitalization steel companies.

The MSCI Canada iShares (AMEX:EWC)
This U.S. exchange traded fund tracks the performance of the broad Canadian market and consists primarily of stocks traded on the Toronto Stock Exchange.

S&P/TSX Global Mining Index (TSX:CMW)
Objective of replicating the performance of the S&P/TSX Global Mining Index, net of expenses.

Claymore Canadian Fundamental Index (TSX:CRQ)
Gives investors exposure to the largest Canadian blue-chip equities based on fundamental value.

iShares MSCI Australia Index Fund (AMEX:EWA)
Results correspond to the price and yield performance of publicly traded securities in the Australian market. EWA is heavily weighted towards commodity stocks.

Claymore BRIC ETF (TSX:CBQ)
Designed to provide exposure to the emerging markets in Brazil, Russia, India, and China. All four growing economies are rabid consumers of commodities.

StreetTracks Gold Shares (NYSE:GLD)
Reflects the performance of the price of gold bullion. Each share represents $1/10^{th}$ of an ounce of gold.

iShares Comex Gold Trust (AMEX:IAU)
Corresponds generally to the day-to-day movement of the price of gold bullion. IAU has a 0.40% expense ratio (GLD is also 0.40%).

PowerShares DB Gold Fund (AMEX:DGL)
Designed to track the Deutsche Bank Liquid Commodity Index-Optimum Yield Gold Excess Return and is intended to reflect changes in the market value of gold. The single index commodity consists of gold.

iShares Silver Trust (AMEX:SLV)
Provides exposure to the physical silver market. Each share represents 10 ounces of silver.

PowerShares DB Silver (AMEX:DBS)
Tracks the Deutsche Bank Liquid Commodity Index Optimum Yield Silver Excess Return and is intended to reflect the changes

in the market value of silver. The single index commodity consists of silver.

PowerShares DB Precious Metals Fund (AMEX:DBP)
Intended to reflect changes in the precious metals sector. The fund holds gold and silver futures contracts.

PowerShares DB Base Metals Fund (AMEX:DBB)
Indexed to the Deutsche Bank Liquid Commodity Index Optimum Yield Industrial Metals Excess Return and intended to reflect changes in the base metals sector. The index consists of aluminum, zinc and copper.

PowerShares DB Commodity Index Fund (AMEX:DBC)
Offers access to the Deutsche Bank Liquid Commodity Index— a rules based index based on six liquid futures contracts on light sweet crude oil, heating oil, gold, aluminum, corn, and wheat.

iShares S&P GSCI Commodity-Indexed Trust (NYSE:GSG)
Rival fund to DBC, designed to provide broad, low-cost exposure to commodities, but tracks different indices and has subtle operational differences. A common criticism of both funds is that they have no current exposure to copper, which many people consider the metal most leveraged to world economic growth.

Market Vectors—Nuclear Energy ETF
Launching fall of 2007
Will follow the DAXglobal Nuclear Energy Index, a modified market cap index that tracks global companies from uranium miners through final electrical generation, to be published by Deutsche Borse AG.

At websites such as ETF Connect and Yahoo! Finance's ETF section, you can learn more about the different types of mining and metals funds including the fund's objective, asset exposure, management, and price history.

Conclusion

As world economic expansion forges ahead, demand for gold, silver, platinum, base metals, and uranium will continue to outpace supply—creating tremendous momentum for mining and exploration shares.

Some even point to the United States's increasing debt levels and excessive money creation as an indication of inflation to come. Historically, gold and other precious metals have risen under these circumstances—another catalyst for junior mining stocks.

Junior exploration companies that discover new mineral deposits and bring them to production with joint-venture partners, by themselves, or through buyouts, are the backbone of our modern society. Companies that exhibit knowledge and determination to locate and expand mineral reserves, create value for their shareholders. These are the same companies that also create great investment opportunities.

Use the wisdom and advice of these authors to seek out and discover the highest quality junior mining companies that offer the best chance for discovery and expansion of reserves. Like any other investment, there is risk and no guarantee of success. But the opportunity is there for disciplined investors who understand the market and leverage junior mining and exploration stocks offer.

Authors featured in *Junior Mining Investor*

Dr. Russell McDougal
www.InvestorsDailyEdge.com

David Morgan
www.Silver-Investor.com

Scott Wright
www.ZealLLC.com

Ken Gerbino
www.KenGerbino.com

Adrian Day
www.AdrianDayAssetManagement.com

Brian Fagan
www.StocksandSpeculations.com

Neil Charnock
www.GoldOz.com.au

Clif Droke
www.ClifDroke.com

Dr. Richard S. Appel
www.FinancialInsights.org

James Finch and Julie Ickes
www.StockInterview.com

Jason Hommel
www.SilverStockReport.com

Dudley Baker
www.PreciousMetalsWarrants.com

Roland Watson
www.SilverAnalyst.blogspot.com

Websites

www.kitco.com

www.goldseek.com

www.gold-eagle.com

www.gold-seeker.com

www.silverseek.com

www.mineweb.com

www.uraniumseek.com

www.silverminers.com

www.resourceinvestor.com

www.minesite.com

www.321gold.com

www.thebulliondesk.com

www.infomine.com

www.kitcocasey.com

www.etfconnect.com

www.canadianinsider.com

www.hardassetsinvestor.com

www.miningweekly.co.za

www.uranium-stocks.net

www.financialsense.com

www.mineralstox.com

www.tsx.com

www.stockhouse.com

www.butlerresearch.com

www.clivemaund.com

www.speculative-investor.com

www.theaureport.com

www.miningsectorstocks.com

www.asx.com

www.investmentu.com

Publications and Media

Resource World Magazine
www.resourceworld.com

Smartstox – industry news and interviews
www.smartstox.com

Mining Journal
www.mining-journal.com

The Northern Miner
www.northernminer.com

Korelin Economic Report
www.kereport.com

Canadian Mining Journal
www.canadianminingjournal.com

StockWatch – news and real time quotes
www.stockwatch.com

Mineral Titles Online – stake a claim in B.C.
www.mtonline.gov.bc.ca

Reports on Business Television
www.robtv.com

Books and References

Gold Rush: Inspiring Stories of More Than 25 Companies in Search of the World's Most Precious Metal, by Michael Caldwell, Creative Classics Inc., 2005

The Ultimate Gold Stock Trader: The Professional's Guide to Trading, Speculating and Investing in Gold Stocks, by Reg Ogden, PBS Publishing Company, 2005

Investing in the Great Uranium Bull Market: A Practical Investor's Guide to Uranium Stocks, by the Editors of StockInterview, a Publication of StockInterview, 2006

Resources Rock: How to Invest in the Next Global Boom in Natural Resources, by Malvin Spooner with Pamela Clarke, Insomniac Press, 2005

The Investor's Guide to Penny Mining Stocks, by Robert Bishop, KCI Communications, Inc., 1987

Silver Bonanza: How to Profit from the Coming Bull Market in Silver, by James U. Blanchard and Franklin Sanders, Jefferson Financial, Inc., 1993

Investing in Gold: How to Own it, How to Profit from it, by Jonathan Goodman, Ned Goodman and Steven G. Kelman, Key Porter Books Limited, 1992